Birding
for
Everyone

Encouraging People of Color
to Become Birdwatchers

John C. Robinson
Foreword by Kenn Kaufman

WINGS-ON-DISK

Birding for Everyone
Encouraging People of Color to Become Birdwatchers

For information, or to order additional copies of this book, please contact:

WINGS-ON-DISK
5055 Business Center Drive
Suite 108, PMB 110
Fairfield CA 94534
www.onmymountain.com/presspage

PUBLISHER'S CATALOGING-IN-PUBLICATION DATA

Robinson, John C.
    Birding for everyone : encouraging people of color to become
birdwatchers / John C. Robinson. -- 1st ed. -- Fairfield, CA : Wings-on-
Disk, 2008.
        p. ; cm.
    ISBN: 978-0-9679338-3-2 (pbk.)
    Includes bibliographical references and index.
    1. Bird watching--Amateurs' manuals. 2. African Americans--
Recreation. 3. Minorities--Recreation. I. Title.
    QL677.5 .R63 2008   2006940699
    598.072/34--dc22   0801

4 6 8 9 7 5

Credits and Permissions

Acknowledgments

Birding for Everyone is the largest book project I have ever completed. Given the scope of the project, it was impossible for me to accomplish all the research tasks on my own. I am forever grateful for the assistance provided by a number of key individuals whom I would like to acknowledge here.

First and foremost are my mother, Aleise F. Robinson, who always encouraged me to learn more about this planet we live on; and my wife, Marlene, who has given me more than she will ever know. Moreover, I must note that birding with David Nkosi in South Africa during March 2006 renewed my unbridled enthusiasm for birds and nature.

I also wish to acknowledge Aubray G. Starks for sending me the first surveys; Kenn Kaufman, Ted Eubanks, and Paul J. Baicich for recognizing and championing the motivation within me; Gary Worthington and Don Kodak for showing me the path; and the U.S. Fish and Wildlife Service, U.S. Forest Service, American Birding Association, National Audubon Society, Fermata, Inc., East Bay Nature of Walnut Creek - California, Gary Green, Ken Cordell, Becky Stephens, Teresa Benson, and Bob Barnes for their significant contributions to this effort. Sam Cuenca, Keith Russell, Les Chibana, Carlotta Hargrove, Gabino Garcia, and LaToya Mabry each shared their story to serve as inspiration to countless others. I also received invaluable assistance and encouragement from Sal Glynn, C. J. Ralph, Rosemary Stefani, Ted Floyd, Lynn Tennefoss, Greg Butcher, Mike Sellors, Bob Hargis, Samuel Smith, and Audrey Peterman. Photographer James D. Northey, Karala Northey, Sarah D. Gill and the Richardson Bay Audubon Center; and Charles Page, Gwen Page, Safirah Majid, and Tariq Majid joined me on a cold January morning in 2007 to create the front cover I always dreamed of.

Many, many unnamed persons contributed to the surveys that produced the data without which this book would not exist; I thank all of these people for their efforts.

Ultimately, however, this book is dedicated to Thomas Cleaver, Jr., who changed the lives of so many children while he was with us, and who, through this book, will change the lives of so many more.

Contents

Birding for
Everyone

Foreword

THOSE OF US WHO ARE BIRDERS should be the first to acknowledge that diversity is a good thing. We crave diversity, admire it, go to great lengths to experience it. In the backyard, we may be pleased to have scores of goldfinches on the thistle-seed feeders, but still we'll put out other foods to try to attract cardinals, juncos, nuthatches, and chickadees. We may have seen a hundred species of birds already, but we'll scour the woods and shorelines for just one more. When we get into birding competitions, the goal is always to see more different kinds, not just more individuals. For birders, variety is not just the spice of life, it's the main course.

Considering that, it is ironic that diversity within the birding community itself has been a long time coming. I have been actively birding since I was six years old, but I was in my twenties before it began to dawn on me that the birders I met all seemed to be cut from the same white cloth. And the point really hit home when I started to do a lot of public speaking. Time after time I would go to speak to large audiences at birding events in places like Alabama or New Jersey or Michigan, and see not one African American in the room. I would speak to birding groups in Arizona or New Mexico or California, and see no Native Americans and scarcely anyone of obviously Hispanic or Asian background. The lack of diversity was striking and disturbing. The birders I met all seemed open and friendly, as if they would welcome anyone into their midst; but for some reason, large segments of the populace were just not there.

In decades past, when birding was largely a local activity, it was possible to overlook the homogeneous makeup of the participants. But with the greatly increased communication and travel of the 1990s, finally became obvious on a large scale. Not so obvious was what we could do about it. As a modest effort on this front I arranged to have my *Kaufman Field Guide to Birds of North America* translated and published

xvi Birding for Everyone

in Spanish. I have many friends of Hispanic descent who speak English better than I do, but census results indicate that there are millions of Americans who are more comfortable in Spanish than in English. My hope was that the Spanish bird guide would help to lure more of them into the field.

A bigger challenge was figuring out a way to welcome more African Americans into birding. This is an era when we are seeing more and more African Americans assuming leadership roles in many arenas, from politics to science to business, making it all the more perplexing that they are mostly missing from the birding community.

Of course there are some brilliant exceptions, and one of the stars among them is my friend John C. Robinson. A top-notch birder who has worked as a biologist and started his own software company, John refuses to be limited by stereotypes and refuses to settle for the status quo. While most of us have just talked about the lack of minority participation in birding, John has been doing something about it, actively researching the problem with surveys and interviews. In this book he pulls together the results of his research and lays out a positive view of the future for the benefit of us all.

Birding For Everyone is an extremely important book. It is appearing at a critical time, when there is increased focus on enhancing access to the outdoors for all people, especially for children. This is a critical time for bird conservation as well. If we are going to have birds to watch in the future, birds and their habitats need all the friends they can get, from all the communities and cultures of people in the US and around the world. So this book has the potential to improve the future for both people and birds.

Therefore, I applaud John Robinson for writing *Birding For Everyone*, and I heartily recommend this book to everyone involved with nature study, conservation, outdoor recreation, and environmental education. Thanks to John's efforts, I have a renewed hope that on future field trips I will be able to enjoy not only a diversity of birds, but a beautiful and satisfying level of diversity among my fellow birders as well.

Kenn Kaufman

Introduction

IMAGINE YOU ARE A BIRDWATCHER standing in a parking lot at the trailhead leading to a forested woodland. It is an early May morning and the peak of the spring bird migration is happening. The woods in front of you are alive with the chirping and warbling of Louisiana Waterthrushes, Kentucky Warblers, Acadian Flycatchers, Hooded Warblers, and Pileated Woodpeckers, to name a few.

You glance over your shoulder, searching for someone to share in your rising anticipation. There's no one around. You turn your attention to yourself. Hiking boots are properly laced up and pant cuffs tucked into socks to keep out ticks and other biting insects. Your binoculars are glistening from last night's cleaning, and a copy of Kenn Kaufman's *Birds of North America* hangs in a belt pouch at your side. The melodious songs of the birds continue to erupt from the forest. You are ready to spend the next few hours hiking through these woods in search of the magical birds inside.

The birds attempt to out-sing and out-display their nearest neighbor. "Ba-dee, Ba-dee, Ba-dee, phe-blee!" goes the song of the Hooded Warbler,   its voice echoing from a wet ravine on the northeast edge of the forest. The cacophony of singing draws you to the forest and the bright shades of green produced by the growth of new leaves ready to soak up the sun all day long.

Hooded Warbler

What you need is the permission to begin birding. But when will someone come along and give you that permission, or perhaps even accompany you and assist in identifying the birds found there? How long will you have to wait?

Most mainstream birders go birding when they want. They never ask permission. The above circumstances may seem extreme, but I call attention to them to make a point: many beginning birdwatchers, especially people of color, would like to go birding, yet rarely ask for assistance. Instead, as Thomas Cleaver, Jr. explained to me during a telephone call in fall of 2003, they wait for chance to offer them the opportunity.

The purpose of *Birding for Everyone* is to explore the lack of minorities among birdwatchers, reasons for the relative absence of minorities among birders, and effective solutions as part of outreach and recruitment programs. Thomas Cleaver, Jr., was known as "a master naturalist, avid gardener and birdwatcher [who] used those interests to teach others, particularly inner city youngsters, to appreciate nature and sports." Many of the kids he worked with were African American and Hispanic. Carlotta Hargrove, who helped Thomas establish a youth program with the San Antonio Parks and Recreation department, remains active in the program today. Together, Thomas and Carlotta helped inner city youths of San Antonio to learn the importance of setting and reaching goals through activities such as tennis, Tae Kwan Do, and birding.

When Thomas heard of my research, he offered to help. I remember being on the telephone with him that day, talking about the kids he and Carlotta worked with. An inner-city youngster's growing interest in nature and the outdoors can be easily silenced. Many of the kids wanted to go birding, but didn't know how to ask. I understood immediately. If someone never asked me for help to learn more about an activity, I'd assume she had no interest. Thomas described this phenomenon in more detail: "We have at least five teens and five 10 to 13 year olds who are experienced birders. As they age into their teens, they tend to lose self-actuated motivation to be actively involved, that is, they will go birding but they rarely ask to go."

The kids who enrolled in the birding program Thomas and Carlotta offered were called the Fairchild Warblers. The Fairchild Warblers competed in the Great Texas Birding Classic each year. In 2002, I collaborated with the Brunton Binocular Company to sponsor the Fairchild Warblers. All of the hard work paid off, and the Fairchild Warblers won in the Great Texas Birding Classic on their third try. This inspired an even younger group of kids to do the same thing. This is one example of role models at work. Thomas was a role model for the kids, and the kids were role models for younger kids.

Based on our conversation in 2003, Thomas and I agreed to work together on this book. I planned to contact him when I needed the chapters featuring his work and the kids' accomplishments. In March 2005, I sent an email to Thomas only to find his email address no longer valid. Believing I could find an alternate address for him, I did a Google search on the Internet for "bird Thomas J. Cleaver, Jr." and was deeply saddened by the results.

I found a Web site containing a tribute to Thomas J. Cleaver, Jr. He died in a car accident at the age of fifty-seven on September 15, 2004. The tribute stated, "No man ever stands so tall as when he stoops to help a child." I knew at that very moment that my book must be dedicated to Thomas Cleaver, Jr. and the work that he did.

Harry Noyes, vice president of the Bexar Audubon Society in San Antonio, Texas, recently wrote to me about a conversation he had with Thomas Cleaver. "I have long been bothered by the low number of minority-group members involved in conservation-related activities. In fact, I once discussed this very briefly with Thomas Cleaver. He acknowledged the challenge and offered no magic answers as to how we could get more minorities involved, but I think his work was part of the answer. That is, he was growing a new generation of young Blacks and Hispanics who would love birding and hopefully would carry that over into conservation education and action. His death was devastating, not only to so many of us personally, but in terms of the likely loss of that development. He was strong evidence that some people are indeed indispensable. [I knew and] admired him deeply."

Every person I meet who knew Thomas Cleaver, Jr. has similar things to say about him. I am glad I was successful in contacting Carlotta Hargrove. She provided the information Thomas originally promised to give me about their youth program. It is my hope the stories of Thomas Cleaver, Jr., Carlotta Hargrove, and the Fairchild Warblers will inspire others to take a deeper interest in nature and the conservation of our natural resources.

After Thomas Cleaver's death, Harry Noyes wrote a letter to the director of the San Antonio Parks and Recreation Department, asking the director to keep birding in mind when searching for a successor to Thomas. "Tom and Carlotta wanted (and want) something more for those kids who, through physical limits they cannot control, will never collect walls of trophies. ... They want them to experience what it feels like to excel, to be world class at something. Tom realized that birding filled the bill. You don't have to be tall, strong, fast, agile, or coordinated to be a great birder. You don't have to be super smart. The qualities you need to be a top-flight birder are precisely those qualities of the heart that Tom and Carlotta want to foster in all their kids — focus, hard study, hard work, perseverance, and dedication. And the [Fairchild] Warblers have proved the validity of Tom's theory."

Noyes's letter shows the positive influence adults can have on children. Usually in a birder's past is an adult, such as a teacher or parent, who encourages the initial attraction to birds until it grows into a passion. Thomas and Carlotta performed this role with the Fairchild Warblers.

In the case of interactions between adults and children, we seldom consider the possible ramifications. The mind of a child is waiting to be filled with knowledge and information. What they learn at this time in their lives comes from the teachings of the adults. When children are exposed to the natural world, they become conditioned to see the outdoors as an important part of their lives. After the conditioning has been set in the subconscious mind, it is very difficult to change. Imagine explaining the merits of studying nature and the outdoors to an adult who was never conditioned to enjoy or experience it as a child!

Children and young adults need to feel what it is like to be a winner, to set a goal, see themselves in possession of the goal, and perform the activities that result in achieving the goal. Sir Edmund Hilary did not reach the summit of Mt. Everest on his first attempt. He failed in

1951, and again in 1952. On his third try in May 1953, Sir Edmund and Tenzing Norgay were the first to reach the summit and make it back down alive. Likewise, the Fairchild Warblers were able to win in the Great Texas Birding Classic on their third attempt. Goal setting and achievement are important to the self-esteem and future development of inner-city youth. Thomas Cleaver, Jr., and Carlotta Hargrove understood this very well. If we as a society fail to practice goal setting and achievement in our schools and community programs, we do a disservice to the children and young adults who depend on us to teach them about the world.

The lack of minorities among birdwatchers and other outdoor recreation and nature-oriented groups has garnered increasing interest in recent years. This is the reason why *Birding for Everyone* has been written. With simple adjustments to our educational and sociocultural infrastructure, positive changes can be effected that will encourage a greater number of people from diverse ethnic and racial back-   grounds to take up an interest in the outdoors.

Birding for Everyone is about understanding how that can be accomplished.

Yellow-headed Blackbird

Chapter 1

The Making of a Birdwatcher

*Downy
Woodpecker*

A "DOWNY" WHAT? Why would anyone give such a name to a bird? My housemate Kim anxiously pointed out the kitchen window to the snow-covered yard where a weathered bird feeder sat on top a metal pole. The wooden rectangular bird feeder slightly tilted to one side, with snow piled on the feeder's roof. The tiny yard was lined with small trees and shrubs, and a few were close to the feeder itself.

I followed Kim's finger and I saw it clinging to the feeder, a black and white bird with a small patch of red on its head. "That's a Downy Woodpecker," she said.

I knew what a woodpecker was, Saturday morning cartoons not being a complete waste of time, but why "downy"? Images of fabric softener bottles came to mind and I could not make any useful connection between washing clothes and identifying a woodpecker.

This happened during January 1979. I was living in Ames, Iowa, and had recently moved from the college dormitories at Iowa State University to a small two-bedroom house near campus. Kim was a fellow student in fisheries and wildlife biology. I was about to take my first class in a course called "Ornithology," the study of birds.

I had not planned to follow birds. My college years were a preparation for my ultimate career goal, the study of wolves in the Canadian and Alaskan arctic. Why did I find myself so intrigued by that Downy Woodpecker? Even an experienced birder admires the contrast of softness (downy) with hardness (the chisel-like bill of the woodpecker) embodied in the bird's name.

As a young child in Pittsburgh, Pennsylvania, my fondness for school was nearly nonexistent. School was an interruption of the time better spent with my parents, my brother Carter, and my sister Eva Marie. Not until the fourth grade did I take an interest in achieving good grades. As late as the sixth grade, my reading was limited to those materials I needed as part of homework or in-class assignments.

The school librarian, Mrs. Avalon, noticed my lack of enthusiasm for reading. She approached me and asked about my interests. The outdoors, I replied, and stories of exploring unknown lands. She suggested *Big Red* by Jim Kjelgaard, the story of an Irish setter dog. Mrs. Avalon asked me about the book when I returned it and I told her of my excitement. She recommended Kjelgaard's two sequels, *Outlaw Red* and *Irish Red*. I accepted her offer and suddenly became a reader. I hurried back to the school library for more books.

Little did I realize the significance of the gift Mrs. Avalon gave me. I changed from an indifferent reader to someone whose fascination with the outdoors was encouraged by the magic of fiction. Mrs. Avalon suggested books by a different author.

The author was Jack London, and the books were *Call of the Wild* and *White Fang*. My worn copy of *White Fang* still sits on my bookshelf, nearly thirty five years later. The image I created of myself as an adult from reading London was to be a biologist on the arctic tundra studying the timber wolf. By the eleventh grade, I'd spent five years working on that image and fostered it with other reading.

I set a simple ground rule when I began to think about college: my career must be something I enjoy. The establishment of this rule was significant and I took the next step by considering what I wanted to do for a living.

I thought hard, then began to worry. I thought and worried some more. Only one thing stood out. I wanted to be a wildlife biologist.

I applied to several schools with wildlife degree programs, and was accepted at Iowa State University as a freshman in its fisheries and wildlife curriculum. During my first eighteen years, I had lived in the middle of a big-city life. I had never taken a camping trip, visited a wildlife refuge or national forest, or worked on a farm. But I had my image, thanks to Jack London.

For the first two years of college, I read about wolves and even went on an extended weekend trip to northern Minnesota for a seminar on the interactions between wolves, moose, and deer.

I could identify cardinals, robins, and crows, but was lost if someone asked me the difference between a grackle and a starling. I never pondered such things. In January 1979, Kim and I reviewed the courses I would take in the spring.

"What is this ornithology course?" I asked her.

"It's the study of birds," she patiently replied.

The course was needed in order to obtain my degree. It was mandatory. Within a university, "mandatory" and "unfamiliarity with a topic" combine to make any student wonder how much she or he will have to study in order to receive a passing grade. Kim recognized my discomfort and motioned me to the kitchen window.

"You see that bird?" she asked. "That's a Downy Woodpecker."

The name took me by surprise. How can a "downy" bird drill deep holes inside the trunk of a tree?

I stood watching the woodpecker as Kim explained how I would learn all about the bird and many others when I took the ornithology class in the spring.

The spring quarter came. The course was a combination of lecture and laboratory classes. I was assigned my first pair of binoculars, an inexpensive lens capable of only 6× magnification. One regularly scheduled lab class included a trip to the local city park, where I made a startling discovery.

For a teacher, once a year (or every several years) a student comes along with the ability to immerse himself into the subject matter and become one with it. During our first field trip, our lab instructor, Nick Rodenhouse, showed us how to use the binoculars and adjust them to fit our eyes. He then led us down several trails, stopping whenever he found a bird he could point out to us and tell us how to identify it. I recognized what he was doing and focused on the surrounding environment, and began to see the birds as live fruits hanging from the trees and shrubs. By the end of the field trip, I began to point the birds out to Nick who brought them to the attention of the other students. He told me that my ability to see their subtle movement among the leaves was already well developed.

The lecture portion of the course, taught by Dr. James J. Dinsmore, was no less amazing for me. Perhaps the most memorable event in one of the first lectures was the instructor telling us that over 8,600 species of birds exist in the world. My understanding of the world had been tipped on its side, turned on its ear, and spun around. I was shocked by how little I knew about the world. How had I gone through twenty years of living without recognizing the many species of birds around me? I set a goal to learn more about all of these birds.

Each week I immersed myself in ornithology. Dr. Dinsmore asked us to learn not only the academic content of the course, which was part of a one-hour lecture two times a week, but also to recognize birds by sight and sound. We were tested on our capability in these areas during each exam. In addition, each student was asked to initiate and complete a study of the bird life in or around the college campus and submit a written report. This assignment frightened me. I began to realize the amount of knowledge I had to assimilate, and what a daunting task was ahead.

We studied the waterfowl of North America during the first weeks. The male duck of most species was easy to recognize, while most females were mottled brown in color and I wondered how I would be able to identify them in the field. We then turned our attention to the sparrows. Those little brown birds were ten times more difficult to identify than waterfowl. Weekly field trips took us to local areas and we studied the birds in real life, concentrating on those species recently introduced in the lab.

I was a quarter of the way through the course when the transformation took place. Some people liken the transformation to catching a disease, others to acquiring an addiction, and most agree there is rarely a cure. I had become a birdwatcher.

Song Sparrow

I hunched over the pages of the field guide, beginning with the loons and ending with the sparrows, reading about birds I had seen or hoped to see. I did this so often I became a walking index for the field guide. Name a bird and I could tell you what page the bird was on. I dreamed about birds, and my most recurring dream was about a Magnificent Frigatebird that magically appeared in central Iowa and flew down the main street of town, on the west side of the college campus. The dream never became reality, but I still remember its vividness.

The comprehensive final exam came after eleven weeks of course content and associated field trips. I had completed my independent field study of birds around the college campus, in which I looked at the difference between the birds found in evergreen forests as compared to deciduous forests. We had to review all of the class lecture notes for the final exam, and be able to recognize any of the North American bird species we had studied in the laboratory as well as some we had never seen before. We also were required to know about sixty-four different bird songs.

My enthusiasm for the course was my guiding angel. I studied hard and entered the laboratory portion of the final exam with excitement and trepidation. As I went from one question to the next, the excitement rose and the trepidation correspondingly dissipated. Some questions had a stuffed specimen of the bird on display, and we were asked to identify it or answer questions about its biology. Each question had a nugget of wonderful information attached to it.

I missed a few questions, but got most of them correct. The laboratory final exam was complete. However, the exam for the academic / lecture content was yet to come. I studied some more, and the day came when I walked into the classroom to take that last hour-long exam. During that hour, it seemed as if a mist rolled into the classroom. The mist was looking for something, or someone. It finally found me and I was engulfed. The mist was ornithology. I was enveloped by a sense of wonder and amazement as I worked through the exam. The end of the hour neared and these sensations reached a crescendo. I marked my last answer, gathered my papers, and walked down to meet Dr. Dinsmore.

The mist was about birds. It brings tears to my eyes thinking about this. I had immersed myself in their world for eleven weeks. I had studied them, learned their songs, discovered their beauty, and now the course was ending. How can anything end during the month of May, in the springtime? It did not seem possible this should be so. It was warm outside. Birds were everywhere, singing and flying. They were to be enjoyed.

As I handed my exam to Dr. Dinsmore, I was sad the ornithology course was over. It had been so much fun. Turning in the final exam for other courses meant it was time to study other subjects. Ending this course felt terribly wrong and tugged at every instinct. The answer to my dilemma suddenly became clear. All I had to do was open one more door. I walked out of the classroom and resolved to continue my study of birds. The ornithology class had only just begun. This is how I found my passion in life.

During the summer of 1979, I took a job studying the waterfowl of northern Minnesota near the town of Bemidji. I worked with colleagues to catch, place leg bands on, and release young ducklings on the many lakes in the area. Afternoons were spent searching for a suitable lake and notifying the residents we would be out on the water in the evening with a boat and spotlight. We began our work in earnest at nightfall, then returned home and slept from 6:00 a.m. to 1:00 p.m. The cycle repeated itself the next day.

This daily routine was different for me because I had been transformed. Not even the lack of sleep could stop my interest in birds. Every morning after returning from a night spent in the darkness on a northern Minnesota lake, I ran into the woods with binoculars in hand to study the birds at Lake Bemidji State Park. I stayed for two or three hours and learned the songs of the Yellow-throated Vireo, and was surprised with glimpses of birds I had never seen before, like the Western Kingbird. Sometimes I escaped to a spruce bog to hear the drawn-out song of the Winter Wren and watch the wood warblers that breed in the evergreen forests of the Great Lakes region and Canada.

Winter Wren

On returning to Iowa State in the fall, my passion for birding had not lessened. I kept a pair of binoculars underneath my jacket as I walked from one class to the next, ready for use at any time. Whenever I saw a flock of birds that interested me, I would take a minute to study them before scurrying off to class. One day I spotted an odd bird hanging around with a group of Dark-eyed Juncos. I knew this bird was different, and as it flew up into a tree I put my binoculars on it. The bird turned out to be a Red-eyed Vireo, common to woodlands and forests. November was exceptionally late for Red-eyed Vireos. By this time, they normally have already migrated to their wintering home in South America. This turned out to be the second-latest date for Red-eyed Vireo ever recorded in Iowa!

The winter of 1979 found me studying birds during every spare moment. News of my zest for the birds made it back to Dr. Dinsmore, who invited me to help teach the laboratory portion of his class the following spring. Teaching assistants were always graduate students, so for me to have a chance to perform that role as an undergraduate was an honor. I helped teach the laboratory part of the ornithology course during the springs of 1980, 1981, and 1982. Each year I took students out to the familiar areas where I had learned about the wonder of birds. I relived the excitement I felt as I watched my students experience their first glimpse of an Indigo Bunting, or hear the eloquent and entertaining song of the Eastern Towhee, which sounds like "Drink? Drink? Drink your tea!"

My image had been tarnished. I was going to be a wildlife biologist, study wolves, and live in the arctic, until I saw the Downy Woodpecker and took the ornithology course. Those two events forever changed the image I had of my future. In just one short year, I had discovered my destiny, the study of birds.

What is a birdwatcher? A birder (the two terms are interchangeable) is a term with a fluid definition, and I am not aware of any that is standard in North America or used internationally. Scientists who study birds are called ornithologists, and many can be considered birders. However, many birders have not received a degree in biology or conduct research on birds, and so they are generally not referred to as ornithologists. At the other end of the scale, there are people who occasionally watch birds found in their backyards. These people may not have a field guide or binoculars, and they may never take a trip for the express purpose of looking at birds. Such individuals would never be described as ornithologists, and it would be questionable to even think of them as birders, although some might argue that they are.

For the purposes of this book, I define a birder as someone who, even at a minimum level, is actively engaged in the pursuit of bird identification and study. As part of my research for this book, I asked African Americans to complete a questionnaire about their perceptions of the outdoors and the environment, biology, and birds. Each person who completed this questionnaire was asked whether they would classify themselves as a birder. The definition of a birder, in this sense, was "someone who spends approximately three to five days each month watching birds with a pair of binoculars and a bird field identification guide." Since many serious birders may spend fifteen to twenty or more days each month studying birds, the definition serves as a very broad description of this recreational activity.

Others in my field of study have offered different definitions of what a "birdwatcher" is and I will discuss these alternatives later in the book. As you read more about birds, birders, and bird watching, you may occasionally see the term "amateur ornithologist." This describes individuals actively engaged in the pursuit of bird identification and bird study, but who do not hold a degree in the field or perform formal research on birds. Because the term amateur ornithologist can be confusing, I generally refrain from using it.

Now that you know what a birder is, the next step is learning how you can become more involved in this recreational hobby.

Chapter 2

How Do I Become a Birder?

Bald Eagle

BECOMING A BIRDER is the same and yet different for everyone. You need an innate interest in birds, a minimum set of hardware tools, software tools (optional), some technical references, and a network of friends.

An Interest In Birds

Developing an interest in birds is not difficult. Some have a yearning for the outdoors from childhood, and others acquire it at a later age. Those who grew up on farms surrounded by nature enjoyed looking at birds as teenagers or in early adulthood. However, one of the reasons that people of color give for not becoming birders is that they have no interest in birds or the outdoors. Can we get beyond this rejection? As a young Black male who grew up in cities during the tumultuous 1960s and early 1970s, I believe we can.

Interest in a subject that does not come instinctively or acquired as part of your surroundings, comes from someone introducing it to you or encountering a role model who helps you develop an appreciation. Hunting is one example. Many hunters began by having a friend or relative introduce them to the sport.

I used to see golf as one of the most boring activities in the world. As a young boy, it took no more than five minutes of watching golf on television to know I had no interest in the game. I quickly turned the channel whenever I encountered a televised golf tournament. I ignored newspaper articles about golf, and as an adult, never gave it the slightest consideration as a hobby to pursue.

Then the world of golf was turned upside down by a young phenomenon named Tiger Woods. After learning how to use a golf club at the age of two, Tiger Woods studied the game through his childhood under the guidance of his father. His brilliance as an amateur was unprecedented, and his accomplishments after entering the professional ranks in 1992 are stunning. Tiger Woods' parents are a Black man and a Thai woman. This allows Blacks and other people of color around the world to identify with his accomplishments. Woods became a role model for these people, and for anyone who regularly golfs.

I now find myself scrambling to the television when Tiger Woods is playing. I search for news about Tiger in the newspapers and Internet news sites. If someone asked me today whether I'd consider playing golf as a hobby, I would have to pause and give it serious thought.

African Americans and other people of color rarely meet someone or hear of a role model that can introduce them to the world of birds. If this significant barrier is overcome, thousands (if not millions) of people will join in the pleasures of birding.

Roger Tory Peterson is an outstanding role model for birdwatchers. He was born of poor Swedish immigrants in Jamestown, New York, in 1908. Roger joined a Junior Audubon club at age eleven, and worked odd jobs for pennies he spent on birdseed and a camera. His father, a cabinetmaker, despaired of his son ever making something of himself. Nothing could dissuade the young boy from envying birds their ultimate mobility of flight. He drew birds when not watching them, and used his skill to earn college tuition by painting Chinese designs on lacquer cabinets for a local manufacturer.

Peterson moved to New York City after high school and studied at the Art Student's League. He graduated and took a position teaching science and art in Massachusetts, where he published his first book, *A Field Guide to the Birds* (see bibliography), as a bridge between the scientist and the amateur enthusiast. Other wildlife guidebooks followed on subjects from butterflies to seashells. He developed his own system of identification, the "Peterson System," which remains the standard. Before his death in 1996, Peterson's bird paintings had been shown in dozens of museums. He received twenty three honorary degrees in science, letters, and fine arts, and many awards including the Presidential Medal of Freedom. Peterson was also twice nominated for the Nobel Peace Prize for his role in environmental awareness.

Kenn Kaufman is legendary among birders and has arguably done more to promote the appreciation of birds than anyone else living. Kenn has been called the heir to Roger Tory Peterson. "[Roger Tory] Peterson was my hero and role model from the time I was a little kid," says Kaufman. "And later I was lucky enough to know him and to work with him on several projects."

On learning I was writing *Birding for Everyone*, many people developed an immediate interest in the work and wanted to know more. Conversations inevitably turned to the source of my inspiration and whether I have any role models. My answer is always Kenn Kaufman, whose writings about birding have been inspirational to millions.

Hardware

Once your interest in birds and birding has been sparked, a beginning birdwatcher needs a good pair of binoculars. When deciding on what type to buy, consider the magnification or power of the binoculars, the size of the objective lens (the lens farthest from your eyes when you look through the binoculars), lens coating, overall weight and size, and close-focus ability.

Binoculars advertised as 8 × 40 means a magnification of 8 (the object observed appears ⅛ as far away), and the size (in millimeters) of the objective lens is 40 millimeters across. In general, 7-power binoculars emphasize brightness and a wider field-of-view; 10× binoculars emphasize a larger image at the expense of a narrow field-of-view and less brightness. Magnification and objective lens size affect the size of the exit pupil, which is calculated by dividing the objective lens size by the magnification. A larger exit pupil appears brighter and more desirable; an exit pupil of about 4-mm is recommended.

Coated lenses have an increased capacity to transmit light. Image resolution is improved, glare is reduced, and problems due to reflections are less frequent. While it is not always possible to tell if the lenses are coated, purchase binoculars from a manufacturer and/or dealer who has an established reputation with the birding community.

Weight and size are also important considerations. In general, women prefer lighter binoculars than men. The ability to hold binoculars steady decreases as the size and weight of the instrument increases.

If you are especially fond of woodland and forest birding, the ability to focus on a bird only six to ten feet away will be extremely important. Some binoculars perform better in this regard than others.

There are two basic types of binoculars: roof prism and porro prism. Both perform well in the field, although roof prisms are more expensive. Porro prisms are fragile and likely to develop lens alignment problems if they are dropped.

Good binoculars allow you to observe and study birds in most places and under most conditions. If you find yourself devoting more time to this wonderful pastime, the next step involves the purchase of a tripod, spotting scope, and a digital or 35-mm camera. The camera should attach to your spotting scope for taking photographs. For the spotting scope, you will want to choose between a 45-degree angled or straight eyepiece. The tripod must be sturdy enough to withstand the wind without excess vibration and extend to a height that eliminates the need to stoop over whenever you want to use it.

Software

Before the 1980s, using computer software to assist in birding was virtually unheard of. However, in today's world one could argue the opportunities for computer-related applications that focus on birds are limitless. Bird-related software is an optional tool to supplement your study of birds. Such software falls into one of three broad categories:

- *Encyclopedic information about birds, including their distribution, abundance, and ecology.*

- *Database to record specific details about birds you have seen.*

- *Software used by natural resource professionals and performs one or more scientific/statistical functions on bird-related data.*

These divisions are not mutually exclusive, and software is available that blends two or all three of these categories.

Several CD-ROMs perform the function of the first category. These can be purchased in stores that focus on wild bird related products or nature in general. Several years ago, I created the *North American Bird Reference Book* CD-ROM. This software, which I encourage you to try, is especially designed for the beginning birder who wants to learn more about how to identify birds by sight and sound. A free trial version of the software may be ordered at a discounted price using the order form in the back of the book, or by contacting On My Mountain, Inc. (www.OnMyMountain.com). This software also has an upgrade package that includes database software to keep a list of birds you have ever seen, including specific details about each observation. This software is used by thousands of birders and allows you to experience, in one application, many of the features found in the first two categories previously described.

In addition to bird-related software, you will also want software to connect to the Internet. Going online to learn about birds is becoming more common. You can download species checklists, photographs, sound files, range maps, survey results, and a multitude of other data on birds. There are also a number of mailing lists to join. Once you become a member, you can send and receive messages about the birds in your area. This is also excellent for learning about rare birds found at locations near you. Many of the Rare Bird Alerts that were only accessible by telephone years ago now provide their content on the Internet.

Technical References

For years there were only two choices for field guides: *Birds of North America* by Chandler S. Robbins, et al.; and *A Field Guide to the Birds* by Roger Tory Peterson (see bibliography). Then in 1983, the National Audubon Society released its three-volume set, *The Audubon Society Master Guide to Birding* (see bibliography). The National Geographic Society countered in the same year with *Field Guide to the Birds of North America* (see bibliography). Since then, there have been additional offerings, too numerous to mention here. You now have many good options when deciding what field guide to use.

Beginning birdwatchers should start with a guide that minimizes complexity and emphasizes utility. The best example is the recently released *Birds of North America* by Kenn Kaufman (see bibliography). As you become experienced in bird identification, you can upgrade to a guide that offers in-depth discussion on the variation (plumage, size, vocalizations, color) a species exhibits. There are many specialty guides on the market that focus on a specific group of birds. These may be of value if you develop a keen interest in certain kinds of birds.

Field guides that offer photographs of birds are at first appealing, but be sure to contrast these with those using artists' illustrations. In general, an artist's illustration is more likely to capture all the key field marks than a single photograph.

In addition to field guides, there are the classic reference books, like *The Audubon Society Encyclopedia of North American Birds* by John K. Terres. More recent books include *The Birder's Handbook: A Field Guide to the Natural History of North American Birds* by Paul R. Ehrlich, David S. Dobkin, and Darryl Wheye, and an updated edition of *The Birdwatcher's Companion to North American Birdlife* by Christopher W. Leahy (see bibliography). All books provide bird-related information and data for birders who want to learn more about the birds they have seen and for ornithologists involved in research. The most recent comprehensive reference covering the life histories of North American birds is the *Birds of North America* project. The print version of this project took ten years to produce. Completed in 2002, the *Birds of North America* is available by subscription at *http://bna. birds.cornell.edu/BNA/*.

A Network of Friends

For many people, birding is a social event. Part of the fun is sharing the discovery of a rare bird with someone who enjoys looking at birds as much as you.

Having a network of friends provides you with a companion or partner when you go birding, and increases the chances you will be notified when someone finds a rare bird in your area. Imagine receiving a telephone call at 10:30 in the evening from a friend about the observation of the first state record for Northern Hawk Owl. Aside from not being able to sleep that night, you will treasure your network of friends when you observe your first live specimen of *Surnia ulula* at 6:30 the next morning!

*Northern
Hawk Owl*

Birding Is Different for Everyone

After over two decades of helping hundreds of students and young adults experience the world of birds, I've learned that each person brings their own individual expectations and aspirations when they ask me for assistance. The need for someone who wants to learn the songs and call notes of every bird in his or her local area is far different from someone who simply wants to learn more about the birds found in his or her back yard. Understanding the differences is as important to the instructor as to the student. If you are a novice seeking the help of a more experienced birder to aid you in learning more about birds, communicate your expectations to this person. This will ensure both of you understand your goals and objectives. Your initial experiences with birds and birding will be much more rewarding because your instructor will focus on introducing new things to you at a pace consistent with your needs.

Like any other hobby or recreational pursuit, birding will never appeal to 100 percent of the population. Not everyone who tries birding will stick with it (that can be said for most things in life). But once your interest has been sparked, you will find a birding community full of individuals, organizations, and information centers more than happy to help you pursue your dream.

Chapter 3

Guess Who's Coming to Bird

Pine Warbler

MY FIRST EIGHTEEN YEARS were spent in Pittsburgh, Pennsylvania. I grew up in a Black neighborhood, and was bussed to school in a Jewish neighborhood straight through twelfth grade. As a young boy, I stuttered, and this speech impediment contributed to my shy personality. I was generally solitary by nature and preferred to come home from school to study or play in my backyard. The best opportunities for me to meet people were at school, where I was the only African American student in the classroom.

The speech patterns I acquired were strongly influenced by my schooling and friends in the Jewish neighborhood. When I attended college in central Iowa, there were few African Americans.

If you and I were to talk on the telephone and you had never met me, you would not know I am Black. My voice reflects the twelve years I spent in the Jewish school system. Many of the boys and girls in my neighborhood who were bussed to the same school as I, have traces of

Black speech pattern as adults because they spent more time associating among themselves than I did. My voice is so different from others in my neighborhood, that people have often told me I have a newscaster's (neutral) accent.

In the spring of 1983, I had recently been hired as Assistant Refuge Manager on the Crab Orchard National Wildlife Refuge in southern Illinois. I had to spend a certain number of years on the job, acquire experience, and receive proper training to graduate from assistant to a real refuge manager. One of the courses assistant managers needed to take was the Refuge Managers Training program. The four-week course was held in Beckley, West Virginia, during the month of April.

Being an avid birder, once I learned that I was going to Beckley, I immediately thought of the birds I might see. My thinking quickly shifted to a logical process of identifying birds by comparing range maps of birds and cross-referencing the time of year intersected with the geographic location of West Virginia. Beckley was a great place for birding, except I did not have any knowledge of the area or where to go.

Then I remembered the names and addresses of bird-count compilers published by the National Audubon Society each year in *American Birds*. I pulled out my 1981 Christmas Bird Count issue and looked for anyone near Beckley. I was in luck and found Gary Worthington who lived within driving distance of where I would be staying. We talked by telephone and I told him I wanted to go birding at the end of April when the migration would be in full swing. He encouraged me to call when I arrived in West Virginia.

I was full of anticipation when I drove to Beckley. Having a car allowed me to leave the training facility on weekends to go birding in the local area. The weather was cool during the first weeks and I found few migrants. However, a significant warm-up was expected for my last weekend. I called Gary and reminded him of our plans to go on Sunday. He said he was very much interested in taking me out birding.

The weather was perfect on May 1, 1983: partly cloudy with a light southerly wind five to eight miles per hour, and temperatures expected to reach 75 degrees Fahrenheit. I stepped out in the early morning air and could feel the "migrant urgency." I just knew the birds were migrating! I drove the thirty five minutes to Gary Worthington's house. He waited for me on the front porch of his house with Don Kodak, who was to accompany us. Not until I pulled into the driveway had I given any thought to telling Gary what kind of car I drove, or what I looked like. Remember what I said about speech patterns?

Gary and Don looked shocked when I introduced myself. They had assumed I was white, like other birders they knew. "I've never met a Black birdwatcher before," Gary said. I was just as embarrassed for not giving him an advance warning. After nervous introductions, we decided to take Gary's car and drove to the first of several birding locations, near New River Gorge by Fayette Station Road.

Although I had only been birding for four years, I knew my bird songs and had established myself as someone who knew many of the songs of the eastern warblers. I was able to score my first brownie points with my new friends by identifying the song of a Blue-winged Warbler. The buzzy song entered through the lowered passenger-side window as we sped by the nearby shrub lands at forty miles per hour. Gary and Don were astonished I was able to identify the bird from a brief chirp and put the car in reverse. We confirmed the identity of the songster as none other than a Blue-winged Warbler.

At our next stop, we used our collective birding talents and saw such birds as the Red-shouldered Hawk, Chimney Swift, Eastern Phoebe, Blue Jay, Tufted Titmouse, American Robin, Gray Catbird, Yellow Warbler, Hooded Warbler, Indigo Bunting, and Vesper Sparrow. We had stumbled on a magnificent migratory wave and knew the morning held more promise.

Off we went once more. We entered a small canyon close to Plum Orchard Lake and the car began a steep, windy descent. I peered out my window and spotted a bird off in the woods, only this time it was a Barred Owl. Gary put the car in reverse and when he saw the bird was perched in a hemlock thirty yards deep in the woods instead of being near the roadside, I scored more brownie points.

My crowning moment came at noon. I asked Gary and Don where we could find Pine Warblers, a species I wanted to see and had not yet found in West Virginia. After some thought, Gary replied there was only one place with enough pine trees to attract a Pine Warbler, although in recent times they'd had difficulty finding it there. "Let's go there anyway," I said.

The pines were fifteen minutes away. We carefully walked under the pines and listened for the song of the Pine Warbler, but all we saw and heard were Chipping Sparrows, whose trilling song became quite familiar. We found eleven of the sparrows and no warblers. Our next birding destination took us to the other side of the highway at Canyon Rim. We parked the car and as soon as we stepped out, Gary and Don heard another Chipping Sparrow. But I heard a singing Pine Warbler. Gary pointed to a tall pine and stated, "There's the Chipping Sparrow." I indicated the same tree and said, "No, that's a Pine Warbler."

If you are not an experienced birder, let me explain the seriousness of what I had done. The songs of the Chipping Sparrow and Pine Warbler are very similar and easily confused, and bird songs for one species may differ in other parts of the country. (I lived in southern Illinois and was only visiting West Virginia, so I could not be certain that Pine Warblers would sound the same in both places). Finally, I had just met two strangers and had only been birding with them for several hours. Yet there I was, telling them they were wrong in their identification, and at a place they frequented. What if I was wrong? How would I ever apologize for such an error?

We stood under the tree and listened intently for the bird to sing again. Seconds later, the trill came from the treetop. "Chipping Sparrow," Gary said.

"Pine Warbler," I countered, this time with more confidence.

We saw movement among the needles and our feathered singer was in clear view. Don exclaimed, "John's right! It is a Pine Warbler." The yellow wash across its breast clinched the identification of the bird as a Pine Warbler. As my companions stared at the bird in awe, I was overcome with a feeling of acceptance. Gary and Don, like all birders I'd met in my short birding career, had extended warm hospitality from the time we met earlier that morning. However, the acceptance I felt as we continued to stare at the Pine Warbler emanated from within me. I belonged to the larger birding community.

I have often wondered why that Sunday has remained so clear in my mind for over twenty years. In retrospect, my experience with Gary, Don, and the Pine Warbler made me realize I did not need permission to be part of the birding community. I learned I was already an integral part of the birding community, and my membership in the community started when I first used a pair of binoculars and looked at that Downy Woodpecker in 1979.

Gary and Don told me they were embarrassed about mistaking the song of the Pine Warbler for a Chipping Sparrow, but were grateful I had been persistent in chasing down the songster until we were able to see it. Birders make honest errors and most birders accept being corrected. Proper identification is the core of birding and more important than ego.

Later in the day we stopped at several grasslands along Gatewood Road and heard the insect-like buzz of Grasshopper Sparrows. On the ride back to Gary's house, he and Don remarked on how well the day turned out and what a great experience they had going birding with me. We saw eighty four species, of which twenty were warblers. I was truly welcome to come back to West Virginia and go birding with them anytime. Although I have never had the opportunity to take them up on their offer, I have treasured that day with Gary and Don as one of my favorite birding memories.

If you think bird watching is something you cannot do because you would not be accepted by other birders in the bird-watching community, read and reflect on the story I have told here. Having been involved in the birding community for nearly thirty years, my experience in West Virginia has happened countless other times. The location may be different, but the results are always the same: birders overwhelmingly welcome anyone who wants to join them in the study and celebration of the world of birds.

Take the first step. I'm glad I did, many times over.

Twenty-two years have passed since the above experience took place. When I wrote this chapter, I contacted Gary Worthington, though he no longer lives in the West Virginia area. He was excited to assist me in remembering that magical day. Here are his words.

Hi, John.

I was surprised to see you were an African American when you pulled into my driveway that May morning, for as you have correctly assumed, you were the first Black birder I'd met. What I recall most about you is your 'ears.' Don and I fancied ourselves decent birders and knew our area well, but here you were, coming from southern Illinois, and you could pick out the sounds as well as we could and even better with the migrants. I recall being impressed with your hearing a Vesper Sparrow long before Don and I could sort out the sound. You gave me a pat on the back for correctly identifying a Parula Warbler, which was singing its alternate song, and not confusing it for a Cerulean Warbler. I felt good about that, for you were the 'go-to' guy for sounds.

Don and I would try to get together once a week or so and sip brandy and exaggerate the activities of the week and build legends. At one of these sipping sessions, we both commented you were the first African American birder we had encountered. You became one of our legends. I don't know how much traveling and chasing of rarities you had done at that point in your bird quest, but we somehow equated you with that group of birders. Most of our birding at that time was local, rarely beyond southern West Virginia (I didn't take a birding trip as such until 1990!). You were our first human link beyond printed material to the greater world of birding. And we were pleased we had fared pretty well with someone who knew more than we did."

It is no surprise that Gary has fond memories. Birding is a positive, uplifting adventure and birders are always eager to share their passion with others. Birding is for everyone, including you.

Chapter 4

Why Study Birds?

*Western
Kingbird*

"JOHN, I HEAR BIRDS!" These words come to mind when someone asks, "why would anyone study birds?"

I met my future wife, Marlene, in early 1996. She was not a birder, but did have an interest in the outdoors and enjoyed hiking. Every time we saw each other, I found a way to work birds into the conversation. She recognized the close connection I felt with birds, and one of our early dates included a trip to the DeYoung Museum in San Francisco to view the traveling exhibit of John James Audubon's artwork. Audubon was a famous naturalist who lived in the 1800s and painted many birds of North America.

Marlene began to experience the transformation and caught the birding bug. I helped her pick out her first pair of binoculars in October, and the first bird she viewed through them was a Ruby-crowned Kinglet at California's Henry Coe State Park. In the space of eight months, Marlene became an enthusiastic birder. Our honeymoon was spent in Dover,

Tennessee, where we stayed for four memorable days in May looking for warblers and other birds found during spring migration.

Why study birds? Those who have never met a birder or spent a silent moment with nature and her feathered creatures ask this question. The best answer comes from those who do study birds.

Professional ornithologists do because that is their job. For the amateur, birding can be a stress-relieving activity from the pressures of the workplace or home. It can also bring one's self close to nature and the changing seasons. The beginning of spring is not confined to a date on the calendar. For birders, spring arrives with the first sighting of an American Robin. Likewise, a harsh winter may be signaled by the arrival of southward bound Red-necked Grebes in mid-November.

These are a few of the reasons why many become interested in birds. For me, birding goes much deeper.

On April 3, 1999, the weather was partly cloudy, and the wind blowing 10 to 25 miles per hour out of the northwest. The temperature in the Central Valley of California hovered around 50 degrees, and much cooler in the higher elevations of Yosemite National Park, our ultimate destination.

Marlene had taken a one-year assignment teaching school kids in the valley town of Merced, an hour's drive from where we lived. Due to the long commute, she arranged for lodging during the week in Merced, returning home on the weekends. I had driven down to see her. We planned to spend the weekend visiting the countryside and studying the birds of Yosemite National Park.

Early in the morning, we packed our hiking boots, warm clothing, food, and our binoculars and bird books, and drove to Yosemite. In the distance were the tall peaks of the park's mountainsides, giant boulders set out like the playground of a lost race. The sun was shining and we looked forward to an enjoyable weekend.

As we left town east on Highway 140, we spotted a grayish-yellow bird on a fence line. The traffic was light and we stopped to study the bird's pale gray breast and head, and yellowish underparts. Its bill was short and black, and its tail blackish in color except for the extreme outer tail feathers, which were edged with white. The bird flew out to catch an insect, then returned to the fence line where we had first seen it. We were looking at a Western Kingbird, a member of the flycatcher family. This was our first observation of the species in 1999 and represented the earliest I had seen them in California (they migrate to Mexico and Central America for the winter).

As we resumed our trip, gray clouds surrounded the peaks of Yosemite National Park. "I can see more clouds," Marlene said as we began climbing higher into the mountains. "Let's continue on," I replied. "We can make it over the pass and into Yosemite Valley before snow falls."

Though it was 50 degrees in the Valley, the clouds would likely bring snow at the higher elevations. Such were the vagaries of weather in April and May in the Sierra Nevada mountains.

Our next stop was at Mariposa, to purchase final supplies for our trip. I parked the car at a convenience store on Main Street, and Marlene volunteered to go inside and get what we needed. I leaned my seat back for a five-minute snooze. Pulling my hat down over my eyes, I settled into a comfortable position.

Marlene opened the door and in came the most amazing cacophony of bird song I had heard. "John, I hear birds!" Marlene exclaimed. Those words were like the bird song itself. I sat up with my eyes still closed, reveling in the blanket of bird song that enveloped us. Goldfinches, kinglets, sparrows, titmice, and robins were engaged in heralding the return of spring to the California foothills. No sooner would one song end than another took its place. At times I heard two, three, and even four birds singing in unison.

Eventually, Marlene entered the store while I enjoyed the unique chorus of bird songs that seemed to emanate from all directions. The town was not yet awake and few vehicles interrupted this tranquil moment. Marlene returned to the car and we continued our trip up into the mountains. As promising as the day had started, it ended quickly.

Snowflakes fell before we were halfway up the mountain. They turned into constant snowfall and we stopped to buy tire chains before entering the park. After another twenty minutes of driving, we needed to put the chains on if we were ever going to reach our destination. We began our ascent again, only to be defeated as the accumulated snow depth on the mountain roads reached several inches.

We turned around and began a careful descent. Determined to not let the snow ruin an entire day of birding, we stopped at a walking trail where we spent one hour birding among the snowflakes and beautiful scenery. There were kinglets and several Red-breasted Nuthatches, one of our favorite birds. With nowhere else to go, we returned to the car and drove back to Merced.

In the quiet of her room late that afternoon, I held Marlene's hands and told her about the wonderful feelings that had come over me when I had my eyes closed and she opened the car and exclaimed, "John, I hear birds!" That instant remains as one of the most magical moments I have ever encountered.

I continued to express the enormity of my feelings to Marlene. The words flowed and they were so strange because the depth of feeling behind them was more than I normally share in conversation. But everything seemed so natural, as if these words were meant to be said between husband and wife. I unreservedly told her, "If I should be on my deathbed and there is one last thing you could say to me, I can't think of anything more comforting than 'John, I hear birds!' I'd find peace with those words and know you would continue enjoying birds on your own. That simple phrase will bring back the memory of my time with the birds and with you. I'd know you would one day join me in Heaven. What more could I ask for than to hear such beautiful words?"

"John, I hear birds!" Those four words have had a major effect on me. Part of it was how Marlene spoke, the feminine quality of her voice, but I know the explanation goes much deeper. Knowing Marlene enjoyed the birds as much as I is part of it, and being responsible for introducing her to birding so she could experience the joy on that morning. But much of it will probably never be explained.

When people ask me, "why study birds?", I think about April 3, 1999. Birds are my life. That is why I study them. Each person will have their own defining moment that tells them why they want to study birds. You've heard mine. What's yours?

Chapter 5

How to Identify a Bird: Ten Secrets to Becoming a Better Birder

*Alder
Flycatcher*

NANCY G. HERBERT AND FRANCIS PANDOLFI published their landmark article on "The Growing Popularity of Birding in the United States" (see bibliography). The bird-watching and outdoor recreation industry were rocked by the news birding had become the seventh most popular outdoor recreation activity and the fastest growing. The National Survey on Recreation and the Environment (NSRE) gathered the statistics quoted in the article between 1983 and 1995.

Cordell, Herbert, and Pandolfi estimated that as of 1995, the United States had 54.1 million birdwatchers. Birding had become a very popular outdoor activity in a short time (only 21 million birders were estimated in 1982). Based on these numbers, during the thirteen years between 1982 and 1995, the popularity of birding grew by 155 percent.

The great majority of birders spend time watching birds within or near the comforts and environs of their home. With a little effort, most birders can see thirty or more species of birds in their yard; and some birders, especially those with large yards and diverse habitats, amass over 100 species of birds on their "yard list" in a few years.

Given the above, birding was destined to grow in popularity. In another article by H. Ken Cordell and Nancy G. Herbert published in 2002, "The Popularity of Birding is Still Growing" (see bibliography), the authors concluded there are an estimated 70 million birdwatchers in the United States, with birding remaining the fastest-growing recreation activity, ahead of hiking and backpacking. The number of people involved with birding increased 232 percent between 1983 and 2001.

What Birdwatchers Want

Having spent over a quarter century helping others appreciate nature and identify birds, I have seen this common theme emerge. The needs of an experienced birder are not that different from those of a beginner. Birders at both of these extremes want to appreciate, understand, and enjoy the bird life around them. The differences arise in how this need is met.

There are over 9,000 species of birds on this planet. No one person has ever seen every single species known to exist. Our planet's abundance explains why even experienced birders never stop learning how to identify birds: there will always be birds they have never seen.

Regardless of whether you are an experienced or beginning birder, you can benefit from the information on the following pages. Birding is about the repetition of proper skills and building upon the foundation of those skills. My ten secrets teach a set of skills you can use for the rest of your bird-watching life. Even experienced birders will find information to help modify whatever foundation you have already built and make it better and more productive in your future birding pursuits.

How To Identify A Bird

Bird identification is a combination of art and science. Many good birders who are self-taught have perfected the artistic side of bird identification. However, with a little formal training and an interest in reviewing publications on the subject, any birder can also apply science to the process.

Before there were binoculars, telescopes, and field guides, birds were identified by "collecting." Birds were shot so they could be studied in detail within a laboratory or museum. Collecting birds with a gun used to be standard practice for accurate identification, and so was taking eggs. The modern amateur and professional ornithologist frowns on bird collection as a study tool. This is not to say collecting no longer has merit in ornithology. It is sometimes prudent to collect a bird, especially one never before seen or described in the literature. In other instances, birds wounded by accident (like colliding with a vehicle) may be collected and turned over to scientific institutions, where they can contribute to our understanding and knowledge.

My Ten Secrets

Here are my ten secrets to identifying a bird, gleaned from over two decades of experience in teaching others how to observe and study birds.

Learn to Use Your Binoculars

Familiarize yourself with the parts of your binoculars. The "objective lenses" are the two large lenses on the end of the binoculars; the "eyepiece lenses" are the two smaller lenses you hold up to your eyes. The "focusing wheel" is the central wheel used to focus the binoculars. The "diopter focusing device" is used to adjust the focus of the individual right eyepiece lens, and usually consists of a ring that surrounds the right eyepiece lens. Depending on the model of binoculars, the ring may also be located on the central barrel along with the focusing wheel.

Using binoculars involves three steps: calibrating your binoculars; what to do when you first see a bird you want to study; and what to do if you are not able to locate the bird in your binoculars.

Calibrating Your Binoculars

This is necessary to account for the distance between the eye pupils and balance any difference in vision between the right and left eye.

To calibrate your binoculars: The distance between the right eye pupil and left eye pupil is different for many people. You will need to adjust your binoculars to allow for this distance, which is known as the interpupillary distance. To make this adjustment, focus on a distant object and pivot the two halves of the binoculars. Bring the halves closer together or spread farther apart until you achieve an unobstructed, circular view of the distant object.

- *To account for any difference in vision between your right and left eye, hold your binoculars up and focus on a nearby stationary object in good light.*

- *While looking through the binoculars with both eyes, cover the right objective lens with the lens cap and focus on the object by adjusting the focusing wheel.*

- *Next, cover the left objective lens with the lens cap and focus on the same object by using the diopter focusing device without making adjustments to the focusing wheel. Make sure the image appears sharply in focus.*

When you are finished, note the position of the diopter focusing device. This device includes a scale ranging from "−" to "0" to "+" and may include additional reference tick marks. The best position of the diopter focusing device is the position that achieves correct relaxation of your eye muscles.

You are done! From this point on, as you look at birds through your binoculars, use only the focusing wheel to focus on the object.

NOTE: Make focusing adjustments for each eye quickly or one eye will compensate for the other by forcing itself to focus on the object before you adjust the wheel or diopter. If this happens, the adjustmet will not be accurate.

What to Do When You See a Bird You Want to Study

See where the bird is located in relation to its surroundings. For example, if the bird is in a tree, it may be two feet to the left of a hollow cavity. If the bird is in a marsh, it may be to the right of a stand of cattails.

When you bring the binoculars to your eyes, there will be a brief moment when you lose sight of the bird. An experienced birder will find the image of the bird centered in the binoculars' field of view. However, beginning birders may find that when they look through the binoculars the bird is not present. This is the result of not having the necessary hand-eye coordination needed to use binoculars for birding. If you do not immediately see the bird, look for larger elements of the landscape, like the tree's hollow or stand of cattails previously noted. These elements are much easier to find and once found, it will be a simple matter to locate the bird. By the way, it only takes a couple weeks of practice before hand-eye coordination develops so you can raise the binoculars to your eyes and find birds immediately in focus.

What to Do if You Are Not Able to Locate the Bird in Your Binoculars

If you are not able to locate the landscape elements as a point of reference, you might try to scan back and forth with the binoculars to locate the bird. This is the worst thing you can do. The field of view within the binoculars is more limited than the naked eye. Take the binoculars from your eyes and look for the bird with your regular vision. If the bird has resisted flying away, you will in most cases be able to find it quickly. Once this is accomplished, follow the directions in the previous step.

Patience

Patience is the first thing all birders must develop. Patience will reward you with experience and knowledge. Consider the first time you heard a Red-eyed Vireo up in a tree. You probably did not know the bird's name but its persistent song caught your attention. As you waited for the bird to appear from behind a tangle of leaves, it continued to sing as if taunting you. At this point, many of those without patience would quit and walk away. Stay calm and remain focused on seeing the bird. Your patience will be rewarded with a view of the bird, a familiarity with its song, and the ability to connect the song with the bird's appearance. This experience will pay off the next time you hear or see a Red-eyed Vireo.

Avoid Competition

Most people see birding as fun and approach it as a hobby or, in the case of professional ornithologists, a job. However, when birding turns into a sport, there is the risk of ruining it for others and ourselves. The birder who must be the first in a group to yell out the identity of a bird, or announce that she or he has seen more birds in one day or one year than anyone else, does more harm than good. This behavior makes other birders feel less inclined to continue birding with such a person, and the pressures of implied competition on beginning birders may convince them to give up before they experience the excitement and enjoyment birding can offer. A birder focused on competing with others may become burned-out when the need to practice one-upmanship takes the fun out of birding.

Not all competition is bad. I encourage it in moderation, but the best person to compete with is yourself. If you saw 250 birds last year, try for 255 birds this year. If your first Louisiana Waterthrush of the season was on March 29th last year, try to find one before that date this year. Competition with a friend can also be stimulating. For example, you might want to see who finds the most occupied nests in the county during the current breeding season.

However, if competition becomes the dominant focus of a birder's life, basic skills will suffer. For example, competitive birders find it hard to admit they erred in the identification of a bird.

Always Be Open to Doubt

A familiar-sounding bird may have a different appearance. For example, let's say you are out during spring migration and hear what you think is a Red-eyed Vireo. You patiently wait for the bird to appear and, when it does, you study its plumage to find the bird does not look like a Red-eyed Vireo. You listen again to its song, and yes, it does sound like a Red-eyed Vireo. The good birder will study the field guide and find there is another species to consider, the Philadelphia Vireo. As you study the bird, you notice traces of yellow on the throat and breast, and a slightly slower and higher-pitched quality to the song. With a willingness to doubt your initial identification, you correctly identify the bird as the Philadelphia Vireo.

Identification by Family

The first objective of bird identification is to determine the taxonomic family. When I first started birding, I hauled out my field guide every time I saw a new bird, and leafed through it, starting at the first page (the loons and grebes) and proceeding to the sparrows. Depending on what field guide you use, this may amount to turning 200 pages. For practical reasons, limit the number of species to consider as you attempt to identify a bird.

This is not too hard to do once you know how it is done. Consider what comes to mind when you think of two different bird groups, jays and crows (family *Corvidae*) and sparrows (part of the family *Emberizidae*). Crows, ravens, and jays have large, thick bills, are usually black in color, or have blue, gray, or green colors, and range in size between that of a robin and a hawk. Sparrows are small birds that are predominantly brown or buff in color (but sometimes rufous, gray, black, or white), and have short bills that usually have a conical shape.

Common Raven   *Song Sparrow*

Each bird family has key traits that can be used to distinguish birds in that family from birds of other families. For example, woodpeckers are usually robin-sized birds (sometimes smaller, occasionally larger) that cling to trees, have a dagger-like bill, and are mostly black, white, or red in color. Representatives include the Downy and Hairy Woodpecker, Nuttall's Woodpecker, and Pileated Woodpecker.

Study your field guide and learn to recognize the traits of individual families. Then when you see a bird, associate the characteristics of the bird in question with a particular family. Now go directly to the pages in your field guide about that specific family. Using this process will make identifying birds easier. Obviously, it is best to have a field guide arranged according to the taxonomic relationships among birds. Guides arranged into color groups or by habitat will not be as useful when applying this recommendation.

Bird Behavior

Once the bird has been linked to a family, look for more details to identify its species. Study the behavior, plumage or color, habitat, and any vocalizations. For behavior, the basic questions are: is the bird active and flitty like a kinglet, or sedate and slow-moving like a bittern? Is the bird shy, or does it allow you to approach without alarm? For example, the Louisiana Waterthrush looks a lot like its close cousin, the Northern Waterthrush, but is very shy. If a waterthrush flies away whenever you try to get close, it will in most cases turn out to be a Louisiana Waterthrush.

Other behaviors to note include whether the bird wags its tail like the Prairie Warbler, or bobs the rear part of its body up and down like the Spotted Sandpiper. Does it feed on the surface of the water like the Mallard or dive underneath in search of food like the Lesser Scaup? Does it peck at its food on a sandy beach like the Least Sandpiper, or probe exposed mud flats like the Long-billed Dowitcher? The American Kestrel will perch on a telephone wire, while the Merlin seldom does. Fox Sparrows aggressively scratch the surface of the ground while feeding, like a towhee. Chipping Sparrows prefer to sift through available seeds and other foods already exposed.

These examples help you build your own mental database of bird behaviors. Then when you are in the field, seeing a bird perform a specific action narrows the list of possible candidates for the bird's identification. A bird bobbing its rear end should trigger in your mind the possibility of its being a Northern or Louisiana Waterthrush, Spotted Sandpiper, or Wandering Tattler.

Determining Color

Not all birds are as uniform in color as the male Mountain Bluebird or the adult Glaucous Gull. Many species have different colors depending on the season (breeding versus winter seasons), and the sex or age of the bird. Keep in mind that under most conditions, you will only have a few seconds to a couple minutes to study the bird before it moves out of sight.

For these reasons, learn how to quickly recognize key features of a bird's plumage or the color of its soft parts (the bill and legs). There are several techniques to do this. First, always carry a field notebook, or have one in the car. Use this to record descriptions of birds while still fresh in your mind. Second, describe the bird aloud as it appears to you. Hearing your own voice makes it easier to commit a bird's particular color and behavior to memory. Finally, memorize the parts and features of the bird most useful to identification. These include leg color, presence or absence of wing bars or wing patches, and breast color (Is it streaked or barred on the chest, or does it have a uniform color on the chest?). Look for back color patterns, tail color, and any noticeable features on the side of the face, including presence or absence of an eye ring.

The observant will notice I have described nearly every visible part of the bird's body. This is no accident. By committing this list to memory, it will be easier to run down the elements of a bird's plumage during the hectic few seconds available when a new species lands in the tree ahead of you.

From a scientific standpoint, the best method of capturing the overall color of a species is by taking a photograph or videotape of the bird. Still shots can be enlarged to study the bird in minute detail, and are especially helpful when the species is difficult to separate from similarly appearing species.

Bird Habitat

Every time you see a bird, you begin to build an association between the species and the habitat it prefers. Plowed fields, short-grass pastures, and other open areas with scattered patches of bare ground and short grass are suitable habitat for the Horned Lark. The Ovenbird prefers forested woodland, and loons are found in or near water.

Identifying a bird depends on how well you understand its habitat. For example, an *Empidonax* flycatcher in late June in a wooded ravine points to the Acadian Flycatcher. In a thicket of willow trees near water, the Willow Flycatcher is the species to consider.

There are many habitat classification schemes. You are not expected to be an expert on any of these schemes. Do your best at describing the bird's habitat, given your current knowledge.

Formal research aimed at identifying the specific habitat attributes needed by Virginia Rails allows scientists to focus on what size of marsh, depth of water, and plants are most conducive to successful breeding in the species. However, all the birder needs to know is the Virginia Rail can be found in a wetland marsh.

Bird Songs

Learning bird songs is one of the best bird identification techniques you can acquire. The younger you are and the earlier in your birding career you take an interest in bird songs, the more successful you will be in identifying birds solely by their song or call notes.

Occasionally job announcements appear for bird census work. In order to be hired, you need to demonstrate an ability to recognize birds by song or call notes. Bird census work involves visiting a fixed number of sample points in a limited time during the early morning hours. You only have so much time to spend at each point and travel between them. If you spend five minutes tracking down every bird you hear before you can positively identify it, you can't sample all of your census points before the morning census period has expired.

To appreciate what this means, consider that 70 to 80 percent of the birds documented at woodland Breeding Bird Survey stops are never seen by the census taker. The birds are identified by song and call notes only.

You can record the songs or call notes of a species for further study and as aid in identification. A good hand-held tape recorder will capture the voice of a loud singer, but more sophisticated equipment is needed to make high-quality bird song recordings like those available in my *North American Bird Reference Book* software (a free trial of which may be ordered using the order form in the back of this book). Once you make a recording of a bird's song, you can listen to repeated playback to validate its identity.

Putting It All Together: I Found a New Bird, What Do I Do?

Don't panic. Review all the points discussed so far. Focus your binoculars on the bird and be patient. Don't rush the bird or hurry to get the best available viewing angle. If you are with a group of birders, don't feel compelled to make an instant identification. It can be a humbling experience to yell out a bird name only to find out you were wrong by missing one or two obvious field marks. Have an open mind and consider all the possible species that could potentially represent the bird's identity.

While this is going on, you have probably figured out which family the bird is in, and noted certain coloration patterns of the bird's plumage. This is when you pull out your trusty field notebook and write down the details of your observation. Note the date, the time, and the habitat. Also record the field marks of the bird (the color and / or color patterns of the wings, tail, head, back, breast, legs, and bill), its song and other vocalizations, and its behavior. Once you believe you have identified the species, write why you feel the identification is correct. Cite similarly appearing species and explain why the bird being documented is not that species.

Practice these ten secrets on a daily basis, and you'll soon be identifying birds just like the experts.

Lark Sparrow

Chapter 6

Birding and the Internet

THERE HAS NEVER BEEN a more exciting time to get involved with bird watching. We have greater knowledge about birds than ever before, including their possible links to dinosaurs, and the digital age has ushered in a new wave. Computers and the Internet have forever changed how we experience birds, birding, and bird identification.

Computers give us a means to electronically store, transform, and share information. Prior to computers, we stored information related to birds on field cards or checklists; in handwritten field notebooks, personal diaries, or scientific journals; with notations in the margins of a favorite field identification guide; or with photographs and film clips.

Before computers, the typewriter was used to organize the information on checklists and in field notebooks. Photographic prints were transferred to slides or slides to prints, and recorded songs transferred to record albums and cassette tapes.

We also shared information by a network of friends we called to talk about birds we had seen. There were Rare Bird Alert telephone numbers, where the caller could leave a recorded message about a rare bird they found and listen to the observations of others. Bird sightings were submitted for publication in magazines like *Audubon Field Notes* or *American Birds* (now called *North American Birds*). The publication and distribution of photographs and song recordings and various print media were important to birders. The National Geographic Society made a big splash with the release of their field guide in 1983, accompanied by a record album containing the songs of various North American birds.

By 1986, personal computers became widespread and readily available for purchase by the average consumer. Novels were no longer written on typewriters as authors took advantage of the timesaving and flexibility computers gave them. Database and spreadsheet programs, although simple by today's standards, greatly reduced the amount of time accountants and analysts spent working with budget forecasts. Birders also saw numerous changes.

Today's birder stores information in different ways. We still have field checklists, but often they are downloaded from the Internet, or created by one of the many bird-watching software programs currently available. Palm Pilots and other hand-held devices record bird observations in the field to be later downloaded to a desktop PC. Scientists and field technicians carry laptop computers to record detailed field notes while in the woods studying birds. Word processors, databases, and spreadsheet software packages store personal and scientific diaries. Photographs and film clips can be scanned into digital formats and used in various computer programs, as can recordings of bird songs.

Prints and slides of birds can be enhanced with image-editing software so the altered image is better quality than the original (Kenn Kaufman's *Birds of North America* is an excellent example of this technique). Bird art appears on Web sites as easily as in a neighborhood brick and mortar store, shown by the numerous Audubon prints sold on eBay in recent years. Bird songs are available on audio CDs and multimedia software, an amazing accomplishment when one bird song can take as much as ten megabytes of disk space. Compare this to the size of personal computer hard disks in 1986, which typically had no more than twenty megabytes.

The greatest advance in technology has occurred with how birders share information. We still have our network of friends who contact one another by telephone, but consider the new ways that have arrived in the last twenty years:

- **E-mail** to share rare bird and other kinds of bird-related information.

- **Listserv** (An e-mail list by subscription where you can read the postings of other subscribers and in turn post to them.)

- **Rare Bird Alert** telephone systems automated by computers or have results translated to written summaries and posted on the Internet.

- **Internet sites** where you can share your discoveries and read about other people's birding experiences.

- **Bird observations** submitted for publication in *North American Birds* by e-mail.

- **Birding software** to generate personal checklists.

- **Publication of books** about birds handled by various computer programs. If you can't find a publisher for your finished work, you can publish it yourself on the Internet.

- **Mass distribution** of film prints, slides, and movie clips aided by e-mail, listservs, and Internet sites.

- **Multimedia CDs** with large compilations of bird information, such as photographs and song recordings.

During the winter of 2000 – 2001, birders were surprised by the appearance of a Greater Sandplover at Stinson Beach in Marin County, California. This was the first record of this species in the United States, and the first in either North or South America. Separating this species from its close cousin, the Mongolian Plover, was not an easy task. The Mongolian Plover, also an Old World species, has a history of occurring as a vagrant in the United States, so there was a reasonable expectation to conclude the bird might prove to be a Mongolian Plover. During the process of identifying the bird, it was important to consider the opinions of ornithologists who are experts on the Greater Sandplover. However, the experts resided in Asia, the native area for the species.

If this Greater Sandplover had been seen during the winter of 1979, the observer would have photographed it and taken the film down to the local photo shop to be picked up several days later. The observer

would choose two to four of the best prints and have those dupli-
cated. Once the prints were ready (estimated elapsed time = 7 days),
the observer would take them home and decide who best to contact
among the experts in Asia, and get their mailing address (mail bound
for Asia = 6 days). The Asian expert would review the photographs and
get concurrence from his colleagues, write his comments, and send the
information back to the observer in the United States (3 days + 5 days
shipping time). By the time the original observer receives confirmation
that the shorebird at Stinson Beach was indeed a Greater Sandplover,
a total of twenty-one days will have elapsed.

Let's jump to modern day, where we run the same scenario:

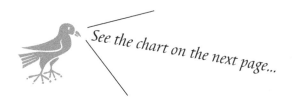

See the chart on the next page...

Description of Activity	Elapsed Time
Bird is discovered; observer realizes he needs to take a picture.	3 hours
Observer retrieves digital camera from home; takes 30 pictures at site of discovery; posts photographs on a Web site his Internet Service Provider has made available for personal use.	5 hours
Observer searches Internet for names of prominent Asian ornithologists; sends e-mail to three asking if they would look at the posted photographs and provide possible identification.	4 hours
One recipient opens request for assistance in her inbox the next morning, reviews posted photographs, and arrives at a preliminary identification of Greater Sandplover. She asks two colleagues to corroborate her findings. They agree, and she documents the rationale used to arrive at the identification and sends the information back to the original observer in an e-mail.	1 day
Original observer opens e-mail and receives recommendations from Asian scientists; lets out a cry of excitement; places details of sighting on Rare Bird Alert hotline, letting others know of discovery.	1 hour
Total Elapsed Time:	**37–44 hours**

What would have taken as long as three weeks in the 1970s now takes less than two days in today's modern times. With such powerful resources at your disposal, why not become a birdwatcher today?

Chapter 7

The Hard Facts

THE DEMOGRAPHIC OF BIRDWATCHERS has become a topic of increased interest in recent years. Discussions on the racial character of birdwatchers are part of a larger concern about the race and nationality of people interested in the environment and its natural resources, within and outside of North America. Concerns have been raised by the National Audubon Society, US National Park Service, Wildlife Society, North American Butterfly Association, and in Australia by Birds Australia, among many others.

The major variable affecting shifts in environmental opinions in the United States is the rising proportion of Hispanics, Blacks, Asians, and immigrants. In fifty years, they will collectively comprise the majority of the US population. Todd Wilkinson, a writer for the *National Parks* magazine, has posed the question: "In the future, if *parks* are not relevant to people, then how relevant will they be to the lawmakers those people elect?" (Emphasis added. Substitute "birds" for "parks."). The political influence of non-Whites in fifty years becomes important from an environmental perspective.

Exploring the role that minorities play in outdoor recreation and their relative prevalence among birdwatchers has been a rewarding and challenging task. Many individuals, institutions, and organizations supported my efforts and anticipated the results of my work. The information I sought was not always easy to acquire, and often only a minimal amount would be gathered after intense weeks and months. Despite these challenges, if I had the opportunity to perform this research again, I would jump at the chance. I believe it is that important.

The focus of this research is to help define outreach and recruitment programs that will enable more people of diverse cultures to find their way to nature through birds. I wish to thank Paul Baicich, the American Birding Association, Becky Stephens, Fermata, Inc., East Bay Nature of Walnut Creek, California, and the USDA Forest Service for their assistance and support in the collection and analysis of the data. In particular, I wish to thank Gary T. Green and H. Ken Cordell, both of who helped organize this investigation and co-authored the first article documenting the results (Robinson et al., at press).

Phase One: The Big Question

Consider the following statement: "I've never met a Black birdwatcher before." I have heard these words since I began bird watching in 1979, and so many times by fellow birdwatchers until I realized there was an undiscovered cultural significance. This began my research into the prevalence of African Americans among birdwatchers.

I initiated my research in 2000 in partnership with the American Birding Association and the National Audubon Society. 322 birdwatchers from across North America were asked how many African American birdwatchers they had met. The average of years the respondents had been birders was 20.57 years and ranged from 1 to 74 years. Roughly one-third had never met an African American birdwatcher; and the average number met by the respondents was 2.38.

Eight reported they had been bird watching for sixty or more years, and had a total of 509 years of bird-watching experience between them. Collectively they could only remember meeting twenty three African American birdwatchers, equivalent of meeting one African American birdwatcher every 22.1 years.

Comments received from the respondents fell into three categories:

What's the Point? Comments said bird watching is an activity African Americans have no interest, or there is no significance to the lack of their participation. Many comments in this category said it is "futile and insulting... to fret and scheme about the present."

Barriers are the Explanation. Comments recognized the lack of participation by African Americans in bird watching and attempted to explain this phenomenon. Barriers identified by individuals included social and economic pressures, and the lack of role models. One respondent wrote, "... once a Black... person admits to being a 'birder', they have broken with the image they are expected to maintain to belong to the Black [subculture], and have instead aligned themselves with the white majority. Being unique in a group you are otherwise expected to belong to is very difficult."

Another respondent stated the insufficient number of role models is "the most important factor" to explain the absence of African Americans among birders.

Call to Action. Comments not only recognized the lack of participation by African Americans in bird watching, but also believe there is a compelling reason to initiate outreach programs to encourage more Blacks and other minorities to participate in bird watching. One respondent wrote that conservationists "expend so much effort trying to expose the majority of our population to wildlife / wilderness experiences in the hopes they will want to preserve it."

Another respondent stated, "It's so much that I would like to encourage more minorities to bird. Further inclusion and engagement in conservation is key to creating sustainable communities."

As part of my research I coined the phrase, the "don't loop," to explain African Americans' level of participation in bird watching and other similar outdoor recreation activities. The don't loop works as follows: if you don't meet others who are engaged in a particular activity, the odds are you will not take interest. For example, very few African Americans carry memberships in local or national birding clubs or conservation organizations.

Because people do not usually become active in bird watching unless introduced by a friend or family member, the low membership rate was highlighted as meriting further investigation. The don't loop epitomizes the barriers African Americans face in becoming birdwatchers. I suspect that many African Americans asked if they watched birds, would say they had no interest in birds or did not understand why anyone would want to study birds. Very few of them would positively say they had ever met a birdwatcher themselves, another example of the don't loop.

Disproportionate nonparticipation by African Americans in bird watching is not a novel phenomenon. Aside from walking and outdoor team sports, African Americans are significantly under-represented across a wide array of outdoor recreational activities ranging from swimming and hiking to downhill skiing and big game hunting.

Phase Two: Survey of African Americans

Periodically, several federal agencies, professional associations, private organizations, and industries collaborate to conduct a survey of the recreational interests of the American people. This survey has become known as the National Survey on Recreation and the Environment (NSRE). The NSRE is not one survey but a compilation of numerous versions of one survey. Each version consists of five sets of questions. Recreation activity participation and demographic sets compose the core of each version and are asked of all people sampled. Three other sets of questions (for example, time constraints, environmental opinions, and African American bird watching) are also included in each version.

Over 80,000 people were sampled in the 2000–2004 surveys. One focus of surveys was the growing popularity of birding. In the NSRE study, a birdwatcher was defined as a person who had participated in out-of-doors birding (regardless of level of dedication to the activity) at least once during the last twelve months. As part of my investigation, in 2003 a set of questions was included that targeted African Americans and African American birdwatchers. The set was designed to answer two basic questions:

What percentage of African Americans in the United States are actually birdwatchers?

What barriers prevent more African Americans from participating in bird watching?

From March through August 2003, 357 African Americans responded to the survey (See table 1), and some very fascinating results were
generated. Only 28 percent considered themselves to be a participant
(someone who watches or studies birds). In contrast, nearly 43 percent of Caucasians interviewed in the basic NSRE survey considered
themselves participants (see table 1). Based on this data, Caucasians
were found to be significantly more likely to participate in bird watching activities than African Americans. Such data further confirmed
the disproportionate nonparticipation of African Americans in bird
watching and other outdoor recreation activities. A 2003 study by the
US Fish and Wildlife Service also found Caucasians to have a higher
participation rate in birding than African Americans (24 percent versus 6 percent). The study also stated 94 percent of birders identified
themselves as White.

How does one define a birdwatcher? The answer is quite variable,
depending on who you asked. Those who have analyzed the NSRE
data divided birdwatchers into three categories based on the level of
participation:

- "Casual" birdwatchers only watch or study birds one to five times
  per year.

- "Active" birdwatchers engage in the activity from six to fifty times
  per year.

- "Enthusiast" birdwatchers spend more than fifty days per year
  watching or studying birds.

Participants were asked to identify how often they spend time viewing, identifying, or photographing birds. Nearly half of the respondents (46 percent) stated they had only watched or studied birds one
to five times per year. However, roughly one-third indicated they were
enthusiast birdwatchers (See table 2), and eighteen of the twenty nine
people who rated themselves as enthusiasts also stated they watched
or studied birds 365 days a year. In contrast, a 1991 study of American
Birding Association members found that half of those surveyed spent
more than fifty days per year watching or studying birds.

The questions used in the study were designed to gather data from African American participants (someone who watches or studies birds) and African American non-participants (someone who does not watch or study birds). For the purposes of the study, participants were considered to be anyone who engaged in such activity out-of-doors at least once in the last twelve months.

The NSRE interviews were performed according to standards set by the National Association of Public Opinion Research. Each participant was asked all questions on page one of the questionnaire (See appendix A for complete questionnaire) and those on the left-hand side of page two. Only one out of every two non-participants was asked the questions on page one, and those on the right-hand side of page two.

Some of the results are directly related to the economics of the bird watching industry. For example, both participants and non-participants were asked whether they feed birds with a bird feeder. Results indicated that participants (39 percent) were more likely to feed birds with a bird feeder than non-participants (17 percent) (See table 3). However, a 1991 American Birding Association (ABA) study found that 80 percent of ABA birdwatchers feed birds with a bird feeder, twice the rate reported by African American birdwatchers in the NSRE study.

Is there a reason for the low rates of participation in bird-watching activities among African Americans? The initial study showed that African Americans are under-represented in local or national birding clubs and environmental organizations. This may explain the lack of opportunity for members of this ethnicity to meet other people who enjoy bird-watching activities. People are more likely to develop an interest in the study of birds if they know others also engaged in this recreational activity.

To test this theory, the NSRE survey asked respondents whether they had any affiliation to a local birding club or other bird-watching organization; or to a national environmental group (See tables 4 and 5). Neither participants nor non-participants stated they belonged to a birding club; and only a few participants stated they belonged to a national environmental group. In contrast, the 1991 ABA study of 1485 member birdwatchers reported "memberships in a total of 163 other birding or ornithological organizations, clubs, and societies … and an additional 121 local Audubon Societies." Respondents in the study also had memberships in 350 conservation societies. For example, 225 were members of the Cornell Laboratory of Ornithology and 909 respondents were members of the National Audubon Society.

African American membership in local birding clubs is essentially non-existent, and only a handful of African Americans hold memberships in national environmental groups such as the National Audubon Society. This further illustrates the limited opportunities African Americans have to become introduced to bird watching.

In another example of the economics of the bird-watching industry, participants were asked about their use of binoculars and bird identification field guides when they watched or studied birds. Over half of the respondents (54 percent) stated that they did not use binoculars or field guides (see table 7). The 1991 ABA study found that 99 percent of ABA birdwatchers used binoculars, and had birding libraries that totaled "157,209 books and 68,497 reprints, or an average of 106 bird books and 46 reprints per person."

Both participants and non-participants were asked how frequently they visited to state parks, national parks, or other similar areas (see table 8). On average, participants reported making more visits than non-participants (11.4 visits to 6.5 visits). Almost half of the non-participants had not visited any of these areas within the past twelve months.

Knowing African American views of the outdoors and the environment, and especially about birds, allows researchers to identify the barriers that preclude African Americans from bird-watching activities. Participants and non-participants were asked about their level of environmental interest, ranging from a general interest in the outdoors, to the study of nature and other living things, to focusing on the study of birds (see table 9). Participants showed a significantly greater interest in the outdoors, study of nature, and birds than did non-participants.

We also wanted to know whether respondents had met or known other dedicated birdwatchers (See table 10). African Americans who participated in bird watching were more likely to know one or more dedicated birdwatchers, consistent with the "don't loop" phenomenon.

In perhaps the most important part of this survey, 100 of the 257 non-birding African Americans responded to the question of what barriers keep them from participating in bird-watching activity. The two reasons given most often were "not enough time" (64 percent) and "no interest in birds" (54 percent); followed by, "no one to go bird watching with" (35 percent) (see table 11). "Not enough time" was the barrier most frequently cited by both participants and non-participants (see tables 6 and 11).

In the earlier study, "no interest in birds" and "no friends to teach me how" were the two most important barriers African Americans identified as preventing them from becoming birdwatchers. Although "not enough time" was not a choice in the earlier study's questionnaire, at least one African American commented this was his main reason for not participating in bird watching.

Over half of the non-participants (54 percent) in the NSRE survey identified "no interest in birds" as a barrier (See table 11). If researchers and environmental educators used outreach and communication to increase the level of interest of African Americans in the outdoors, the environment, nature, and in birds, then this group may be more willing to set aside enough time to become more involved.

Some critics may argue that if the survey had targeted Caucasians instead of Blacks, "not enough time" would have been the top reason for why Whites (non-birders and birders alike) do not go birding or as much as they would like. Why should we be impressed when this reason shows up as the most frequently cited barrier by African Americans? The answer is twofold: first, this is one of the first studies to directly ask members of its target group (in this case, African Americans) what barriers prevent them from participating in an outdoor recreation activity such as bird watching. The responses we received are as close to the truth as we can get, compared to an academic exercise where "experts" in the bird-watching industry sit in a room and theorize what the barriers may be. Secondly, it is significant that "not enough time" is most frequently cited because, upon closer inspection, we see that this barrier can be removed or minimized with the proper education and outreach programs.

My investigation was certainly not the first to look at patterns of participation by minorities in outdoor recreation activities. Dr. Myron Floyd, writing in the *Social Science Research Review* (see bibliography), identified four hypotheses to describe National Park use and participation in outdoor recreation activities by minority populations. The marginality hypothesis supported the idea that lack of income may in part explain the lack of participation by minorities. Likewise, the discrimination hypothesis explained the lack of participation by specific cultural groups as due to experiences with or perceptions of discrimination.

Interestingly, neither lack of money nor cultural differences were identified as major barriers preventing non-participants from watching or studying birds in the NSRE survey. Only one of every four non-participants identified lack of money as a barrier. Furthermore, although African Americans who watch or study birds do not feed birds or use binoculars or field guides as often as members of the ABA (see tables 3 and 7), this difference may simply result from the fact that ABA members are part of a specialized group focused on birds.

One reason frequently cited (and not without controversy) as an explanation for why minority populations exhibit suppressed participation rates in wild land recreation is "ethnically based preferences." Floyd states, "racial and ethnic differences in recreation behaviors can be attributed to different norms, value systems, and socialization practices adhered to by racial and ethnic groups." While the NSRE study neither refutes nor confirms this hypothesis, the results highlight the importance of identifying the outdoor recreational interests and needs of the various ethnic minority groups in the United States. The lists of barriers presented in tables 6 and 11 represent a first step toward this end.

Bird watching offers just one recreational path people can use to enjoy nature and understand the need for natural resource conservation. The opportunity exists to increase participation of African American and other ethnic groups in bird watching (and in conservation) through a carefully constructed outreach program.

TABLE 1. *Ratio of Participants by Race*

	Caucasian		African American	
	n	%	n	%
Participant	2024	42.7	100	28.0
Non-participant	2712	57.3	257	72.0
	n = 4736	100.0	n = 357	100.0

TABLE 2. *Number of Days Viewing, Identifying, or Photographing Birds*

Casual birder (watch birds 1–5 times in past 12 months)	45.8%
Active birder (watch birds 6–50 times in past 12 months)	19.3%
Enthusiast birder (watch birds more than 50 times in past 12 months)	34.9%
Total n = 83	**100%**

TABLE 3. *Percentage of Participants and Non-participants Who Feed Birds with a Bird Feeder*

	Participant	Non-participant
Yes	39.4%	17.3%
No	60.6%	82.7%
	n = 94	n = 104

TABLE 4. *African American Membership in Local Birding Clubs and Other Bird-Watching Organizations*

	Participant	Non-participant
Yes	1.1%	0.0%
No	98.9%	100.0%
	n = 94	n = 104

TABLE 5. *African American Membership in National Environmental Groups and Organizations*

	Participant	Non-participant
Yes	5.3%	0.0%
No	94.7%	100.0%
	n = 94	n = 104

TABLE 6. *Reason That Keeps Participant from Watching or Studying Birds as Often as They Would Like*

Not enough time	61.7%
No one to go bird watching with	25.5%
Not enough money	25.5%
I am uncomfortable because sometimes I feel afraid in forest or other natural settings	23.4%
I feel unwelcome or uncomfortable at many outdoor recreation areas because of my race or ethnicity	5.3%
Other reasons	23.4%
Total n = 94	

TABLE 7. *Use of Binoculars and Bird Identification Books (field guides) by Participants*

Yes	44.7%
No	54.3%
Don't Know	1.1%
Total (n = 94)	**100.0%**

TABLE 8. *Frequency of Visitation to State Parks, National Parks, or Other Similar Areas in Past 12 Months*

	Mean	Median	Range	N	% Not visited at all in past 12 months
Participant	11.4	2.0	0–200	93	30.1%
Non-participant	6.5	1.0	0–365	102	49.0%
Total	**8.9**	**1.0**	**0–365**	**195**	**40.0%**

TABLE 9. *Ratings of Interest in Environment by Participants and Non-Participants*

	Outdoors and the natural environment		Study of animals, plants, and nature		Birds	
	Participant	Non-participant	Participant	Non-participant	Participant	Non-participant
Very highly interested	16.0%	9.6%	16.0%	6.7%	11.7%	2.9%
Highly interested	25.5%	15.4%	25.5%	11.5%	13.8%	7.7%
Moderately interested	34.0%	25.0%	25.5%	26.0%	38.3%	16.3%
Somewhat interested	20.2%	30.8%	25.5%	36.5%	26.6%	30.8%
Not at all interested	3.2%	16.3%	5.3%	18.3%	8.5%	40.4%
Don't know	1.1%	2.9%	2.2%	1.0%	1.1%	1.9%
Average	3.31	2.70	3.22	2.51	2.94	2.00
Total	n = 94	n = 104	n = 94	n = 104	n = 94	n = 104

TABLE 10. *Respondents Who Know a Dedicated Birdwatcher*

	Participant	Non-participant
Know a dedicated birdwatcher	26.6%	8.7%
Do not know a dedicated birdwatcher	73.4%	91.3%
	n = 94	n = 104

TABLE 11. *Reason That Keeps Non-participant from Watching or Studying Birds*

Not enough time	64.0%
No interest in birds	54.0%
No one to go bird watching with	35.0%
Not enough money	26.0%
I don't understand why one would want to study birds	22.0%
I am uncomfortable because sometimes I feel afraid in forest or other natural settings	14.0%
I feel unwelcome or uncomfortable at many outdoor recreation areas because of my race or ethnicity	3.0%
Other reasons	8.0%
	Total n = 100

Cast of Characters

Hooded Warbler male

Yellow-headed Blackbird

Song Sparrow adult, singing

Song Sparrow, Fall

Downy Woodpecker

Winter Wren

Bald Eagle adult

Pine Warbler adult male

Alder Flycatcher

Western Kingbird

Northern Hawk Owl with rat

Common Raven

Lark Sparrow adult

Photo by Rene Thomas

Chapter 8

Expanding the Research

THE FINAL PHASE of my research began in the fall of 2003 and culminated with the publication of this book. During this phase I solicited and received input from birdwatchers representing various minority ethnic groups. The respondents included one Asian person, six African Americans, two Native Americans, one Hispanic, and two who described themselves as a mixture of Native American and African American.

The information proved critical to showing the relevancy of this work to a broader segment of the North American population. The purpose was to learn how minorities become involved with bird watching and the enjoyment of nature, and form ideas about outreach and recruitment strategies to encourage involvement by more minorities. Responses would carry more weight than theories developed behind closed doors in an academic setting.

My small sample size prevents testing for significance in any of the results. However, in the absence of previously published data, I challenge the scientific community and the bird-watching industry to replicate my research on a broader scale to validate or correct the conclusions.

Who provided the incentive to interest you in bird watching?

Usually a parent, Boy Scout leader or scoutmaster, an employer, or a teacher provided the initial interest. At least six respondents stated that one or both parents got them started; others gave credit to a teacher (like an instructor in an ornithology class) or as a member of the Boy Scouts of America. Here are some samples of the experiences:

"As a child, I went into the woods with my mother who dug up the rich, black soil there to use for her roses. She taught me the names of wild flowers, trees, and birds we saw there (in northern New Jersey)."

"My father was an avid outdoorsman; also a biologist and birdwatcher. As a youth, he taught me the basics about bird watching, and the love and interest grew."

"I grew up in rural New Hampshire, the daughter of a high school science teacher. Both parents were interested in the outdoors."

"As a child, my grandfather had bird feeders and bird baths in his yard."

These responses further demonstrate that bird watching is not something people typically discover on their own. Even if they do, another person usually encourages its growth into a passionate hobby.

How did you get further involved in bird watching after the initial interest?

The responses to this question typically involved assistance from schoolteachers, friends, parents, and an employer and colleagues at work.

Consider the following passages that describe the excitement and exhilaration experienced by the respondents as they discovered the richly rewarding hobby of recreational birding:

"I started with basic identifications, like Robin Redbreast, Blue Jay, Large Black Bird; Crow, and Red Bird Cardinal. With experience and God's blessing and many fishing and camping trip opportunities I viewed Canadian Geese, varieties of ducks, waterfowl, and chance of a lifetime eagles. Not only book identification, school involvement, continued family involvement."

"Both parents raised my siblings and me to be curious about all aspects of nature. Bird watching was a part of that. There was always a pair of binoculars and bird identification books handy. As I grew up and started my own home and family in a different part of

the country, identifying local species of birds was important. I have continued that interest and raised my daughter with binoculars and bird books at hand."

"Over a period of years, as a member of the Boy Scouts of America, I participated in summer camps. Working for the bird merit badge started my interest in bird watching."

"I visited the raptor watch on several occasions (sometimes with my partner who I recruited to birding). I made friends with one of the park rangers who encouraged my growing interest in birding and who (although no longer employed there) remains a supportive friend, and leads bird walks I've often attended. I'm basically a shy person, and this essential connection made me feel comfortable. I am not generally uncomfortable around white people, but it was pretty clear that birding is an activity dominated by white people and largely, retired and often affluent ones. I took part in numerous local, out-of-state, international birding excursions with my partner (from Hawk Mountain to Tobago to Spain) as well as going on lots of bird walks with city groups."

"My father's influence continued until I enrolled in an outdoor college. There I was surrounded and immersed in all aspects of activities that cemented my interests in birding. An early course in ornithology, other academics in zoology, association with the college naturalist, and the Outing Club advisor directed my interest. My undergraduate associates in the Outing Club had similar interests at various levels of involvement. The entire college community fostered my interest in birding and the outdoors in such a way that the outcome was inevitable."

Three of the respondents stated that their initial interest began by personal observation. However, when asked to describe how this interest turned into a passion for bird watching, they consistently recognized other people who provided support and nourishment for their pursuits. Consider how they described the process:

"I began going to other estuaries and met other birders who told me to take advantage of an instructor in Huntington Beach, California.

Her name is Sylvia Gallagher. I have taken as many classes from her as I can possibly fit into my schedule. She is the most influential person in my birding career. Now I do surveys, land birds, and am active in our local Audubon chapter."

"Parental guidance and exposure, positive results from bird-watching outings, and the pleasure of at-home bird feeding and observation."

"Growing up I was only interested in game birds, White-winged Dove, Mourning Dove, quail, and turkey for obvious reasons. After being employed by the Texas Parks and Wildlife Department, I was introduced to non-game birding by fellow staff members, which has since led to bird watching as a hobby."

Do you have membership in a local birding club or a national conservation organization?

Of the twelve people who responded to the questionnaire, four stated they had membership in a local birding club, and half also belonged to a national conservation group. Memberships were greater among a sample of 12, which is 97 percent smaller than the sample of 357 performed as part of the NSRE study. This is a clear testament to the influence that other people have on the behaviors we adopt; it is also further evidence of the notion that birding is, at some basic level, a social phenomenon. While many birders go birding by themselves, these same individuals strongly value the opportunities they have to go bird watching with others, or at least share information about the birds they have seen with others who can appreciate their accomplishments.

Membership in a local birding club or national conservation organization can help people remain engaged in such recreational pursuits. A National Audubon Society membership may serve as the initial catalyst for someone's interest in birds. Our challenge is to figure out a way to increase the number of interactions between these types of clubs and organizations and the minority birding prospect.

Do you feed birds? If "yes," do you use a bird feeder? How many times in the last twelve months did you visit a state or national park, national forest, or wildlife refuge?

Eleven of the twelve respondents said they fed birds, and nine of those used a bird feeder. The number of visits over a twelve-month period ranged from zero to 52 and averaged 18. These same questions were also asked as part of the national NSRE survey. Compare the numbers here with the responses received from the NSRE sample.

What basic resources (field identification guide and/or binoculars) do you use and when in your birding career did you acquire them?

To address this subject, I asked the following questions:

How many years have you been bird watching?

Do you use binoculars and a bird identification book to look at birds?

If "yes," how long after you started bird watching did you acquire your first bird identification book and pair of binoculars?

The average length of bird-watching experience among the 12 respondents was thirty years, and 11 use a field identification guide and/or a pair of binoculars, typically acquired within the first 12 months of taking up birding. Seven of the 11 people who used a bird identification book acquired their first book immediately after starting, and the remaining four people did so within the first twelve months. Five of the 11 people who used binoculars while birding acquired their first pair immediately after they started. Four people did so within the first twelve months; one person within the first 36 months; and one person waited longer than three years before making their purchase.

Once the decision was made to study birds, these respondents quickly acquired the basic tools. The significance of this information relates to where wild bird retail stores are located in our cities. Many are not found in lower income, inner-city neighborhoods, yet these are where the non-traditional birding prospects reside. Assuming these prospects can become interested in birding, how will they acquire their first bird book and binoculars? The answer to this question benefits everyone involved, from the first-time birder to the storeowner, the birding industry as a whole, and (most importantly) to the conservation of our natural resources. The more people care about birds and nature, the more they will lobby for the wise conservation of these valuable natural resources while they still exist.

What factors preclude you from going birding as often as you would like?

In the NSRE study, African Americans who were also birdwatchers gave four reasons, the most important one being "not enough time." The other three reasons were "no one to go birding with," "not enough money," and "I am uncomfortable in the forest or other natural settings."

Eight of the 12 respondents also identified "not enough time" as the factor most limiting them from going birding as often as they would like. In addition, four of the 12 stated "no one to go birding with" was also a reason. Only two of the 12 respondents felt "not enough money" explained why they did not go birding more often.

Because of the small sample size of this study, there is no way to place significance in the data with that of the NSRE survey. However, there are two consistencies that appear in these data sets. "No one to go birding with" was cited by at least 25 percent of the respondents in each sample. During my study, one person wrote, "I don't know where to get connected." Outreach efforts ensure a person's initial interest in birding and the enjoyment of nature does not wither due to lack of contact with other like-minded individuals. Anyone who wants to know more about nature or the study of birds deserves the enrichment provided by others who can mentor and otherwise offer encouragement.

"Not enough money," although cited by some respondents, does not hold the level of importance we once thought it did. No matter how busy, or rich or poor, we all find ways for leisure time. It is entirely up to us how we spend that time. Can we decide to look at birds and enjoy nature if we lack the awareness of how this can be done? If we knew, we would make the time to involve ourselves in such activities regardless of how little or how much money we have. This awareness can be developed and supported by the proper outreach and recruitment strategies.

What outreach and recruitment strategies could be put in place to encourage minorities to become involved with birding and otherwise find their way to nature?

Nearly all of the respondents to the study felt it was important for members of the general public to participate in bird watching and / or the study of nature and the outdoors. Here are the reasons given for this belief:

"Our cultures have gotten away from family time. Many families don't leave the house. There's too much distraction."

"The more connected people are to nature, not as found in suburbia, they appreciate what they have and place greater value in its untouched state, and are involved when the natural world is in danger from the actions of men."

"We need people of all races and ethnic backgrounds to understand the importance of native habitats, and the conservation plans necessary to compensate for population growth especially in urban areas. Grassroots volunteers and activists are needed to reclaim empty lots and green them up."

"Support protection and conservation initiatives to pass on to future generations the importance of conservation and the pleasure of exposure."

"Becoming more familiar with the natural world is to value it more and be supportive of efforts to preserve it."

"If you do not experience nature you will not appreciate it or see the importance in conservation."

When asked whether it was important for members of their race or ethnic group to participate in bird watching and the study of nature, nearly all respondents answered "yes" and rationalized their responses typified by the following examples:

"Giving young people alternatives to drugs and inappropriate behavior is certainly important."

"Appreciation, relaxation, and the gift of our surroundings. If we can be aware of the health of our earthly surroundings we can better acknowledge the trouble the human race is in. If the Earth dies, so will we."

"I'm 54, the product of Chinese immigrants, taught by my parents to study and work hard for the American Dream of material things. There was no mention of enjoying life as a steward of the environment, only as a consumer. That was the mentality of immigrants from poor countries."

"Bird watching is a wonderful activity quite diverse from everyday activities and expands our appreciation for the beauty of nature."

"We are all the inheritors of this magnificent gift! We must recognize our responsibility to care for the environment, especially for future generations. The Earth is everyone's home and everyone's responsibility. I would be delighted to see more people of color out birding and participating in nature and conservation organizations. It's a very healthy and stress-relieving activity, as well as, at least for me, a very spiritual one."

"More minorities involved in nature will help form policy as the population grows dominant."

"The study of nature brings a calming effect and serves as a stress-reliever for those who engage in this activity. Bird watching can heal the socially scarred African American."

The respondents were then asked to list what actions they would recommend to increase levels of interest in bird watching and the study of nature among Asians, Blacks, Native Americans, and Hispanics. The responses indicated outreach and recruitment activities should be focused on these five activity areas:

Home and Parents

Much of what a child learns is received from a parent or teacher. In the case of the home environment, the parent has the opportunity to provide lessons to the child about nature and the wise use and enjoyment of our natural resources. In order for this transfer of knowledge to take place, the parent must know it is something worthwhile to be passed to their children. As a result, outreach efforts by conservationists must target the young and old alike.

Consider these comments from the twelve respondents on this activity area:

"Like a lot of interests, there are those that are begun in the home. My daughter now feeds birds, has visited wetlands with her children, and walked through woods with them to pick up litter. Like myself, she has a large collection of field guides, and also subscribes to National Geographic."

"Are we as adults involved? If it were not for my parents to teach me, I would not have been able to teach my children or my husband the joy of watching Red-tailed Hawks and identifying the call of an eagle when out fishing."

Outreach and recruitment efforts must deliver consistent messages about the environment and natural resource conservation on a frequent basis to the homes of people who have not traditionally been recipients (inner city and low-income neighborhoods). They should have content for children, as well as for adults.

The messages can be delivered by print media using postal service mail, telephone, Internet and e-mail, personal visits that canvass a neighborhood, and television and radio advertisements.

Anyone can deliver these messages, but they should be consistent and have a singular, unified voice. Any signs of inconsistency will only confuse the intended audience, and ruin the best opportunity to communicate our conservation ethic with those that have not had the benefit of knowing and experiencing nature.

The birding, nature, and outdoor recreation industry has an obligation to hold summits on this issue. The objective would be to determine the message, how to transmit the information, and monitor its effectiveness.

School

Here is another opportunity to make a positive impression on children. The sooner this is done this, the better. Environmental outreach efforts can start during 10th grade when the child is sixteen, but a long-lasting environmental ethic can be instilled if the efforts begin in the third or fourth grade.

The public school system of the United States leaves much to be desired. Teachers in affluent neighborhoods are often hounded by parents demanding that their children receive all A's on their report card. Administrators are caught between the teachers and the parents, and often find fault with the teacher before speaking out against the unreasonable demands made by some parents. Teachers in poor neighborhoods where many of the children come from single-parent households may not receive as many complaints from angry parents. However, administrators are urged by their superiors to improve the performance of the students and this pressure is sometimes passed to the teacher in the form of untested strategies that lack the proper funding for them to be successful.

Many teachers complain about their thankless job. Many of them go beyond the call of duty and work overtime to get the job done (despite their lowered state of morale) while some do just enough to get through the day. Our public school system suppresses inventiveness more often than it rewards it. As a result, many teachers leave the teaching profession in search of more enriching jobs with higher pay.

I mention this because the opportunities to teach conservation and environment-friendly lessons in the public schools are few given the bureaucratic wrangling taking place on a daily basis. In spite of these problems, there are teachers who find a way to inspire their students about nature, birds, and the outdoors. The teacher, like the parent, must have the awareness to know it is something worthwhile to be passed down to their students. If the teacher does not have this awareness as a result of her own experiences as a child, then the needs and positive benefits of teaching such environmental lessons in the classroom must be brought to the teacher from an outside source. Outreach efforts by conservationists must target the student and teacher.

Consider these comments from the twelve respondents on this activity area:

"Personnel from the Wildlife Federation should visit elementary schools to speak and show birds and other wildlife."

"Teachers of science and biology can schedule trips to natural history museums and forest and parks to identify birds."

"Appreciation begins at school. Start with the youngest and grab their interest."

"Programs in elementary, junior, and high schools can expose children to various aspects of nature and encourage their interest and concern."

"Teachers need to mentor students of different backgrounds and lead them to promote the causes within their families."

"Provide educational products for language schools and churches of Asians. Many attend Chinese language school on weekends. Have outings to local Audubon walks."

"Educational programs are needed in K-12 schools with high numbers of kids from these ethnic groups."

"School-based educational initiatives can introduce young people and their parents to bird watching."

"More school programs are needed to start our kids off right. School administrators and teachers must also be trained so they value the program and carry on its work."

"Community, school, and parent initiatives are necessary. The global village must value the involvement, or our children will hardly develop interests. Some schools get into too much fancy science too early on. What is needed are more hands on, field trip, camping, museum, and experiential nature activities. These would support our efforts."

"Free access to state parks for school groups encourages their participation in activities at the parks, thus exposing the kids to our natural resources."

It is too early to concede that the school system represents the best opportunity to deliver an environmental message, yet these comments are from the same minorities that we want to reach. The concentration of recommendations surrounding schools is very important.

Outreach and recruitment efforts must deliver consistent messages about the environment and natural resource conservation on a frequent basis to public and private schools who have not traditionally been recipients (inner city and low-income neighborhoods). The messages should have content suitable for children, as well as teachers.

Print media using postal service mail, Internet and e-mail, and television and radio advertisements can deliver the messages. The National Science Teachers Association has a membership of over 55,000. Imagine the impact this organization could have if they embraced teaching their students about the environment and how to safely interact with and conserve the environment for future generations. Such a strategy is consistent with the mission of the NSTA, which is "... to promote excellence and innovation in science teaching and learning for all."

This is not to say that there is a complete lack of positive environmental learning experiences taking place in American classrooms. Many examples of success on this issue can be shown. However, the success stories are too few to have the kind of impact that is necessary to effect the change potentially available to us.

Community

Making community activities and programs available that promote environmental conservation is a natural outgrowth of the opportunities that present themselves in the home and classroom. If children are not at home or school, they are somewhere at large in their community. However, children are not the only targets of an effective outreach campaign. Adults can not instruct their children about the environment if they are unaware of the issues. It is not enough to get this information from watching the Discovery Channel.

Consider these comments from the twelve respondents on this activity area:

"Start programs at community centers, parks, and churches to expose older people to nature."

"Support youth activities in such programs as Boy Scouts and Girl Scouts of America, because the tenets are about nature and the environment. Outdoor activities can be for all ages for life."

"Social and educational events can generate interest. Get groups of people together to expose them to concepts and enjoyment of nature."

"Make community needs a national priority and give financial support to conservation programs. There are many community-based programs like Head Start, Student Conservation Association, and Outward Bound, who would assist and support our efforts. There are many that can be adopted or adapted."

"Break the 'don't loop' and support Audubon Centers. Bringing birdwatchers into contact with people who make up the target ethnic group will sever the 'don't loop' phenomenon. Programs such as the Urban Audubon Centers achieve this and must be expanded in scope. If African Americans are not given the opportunity to meet birdwatchers or other outdoor enthusiasts, the likelihood they will develop an interest in bird watching or nature in general decreases."

"We need inexpensive access to state parks."

An effective environmental outreach and recruitment program champions people helping people to enjoy and understand nature. Building blocks such as the Urban Audubon Nature Centers, Head Start, Boy Scouts of America, and Outward Bound already exist. The challenge is how to utilize these and other similar institutions to deliver a coordinated message to traditional as well as non-traditional audiences.

Public Communication and Advertisements

Solutions for integrating environmental learning in the home, school, and community can be communicated through the various public avenues available. Consider these comments from the twelve respondents on this activity area:

"Use public service announcements (PSAs) on television and radio to promote environment programs, also to keep birds, birding, and nature in general on peoples' minds."

"Promote wise conservation practices on English and ethnic radio and television stations. Have minority actors in ads so minorities can identify with the cause."

"Generate publicity on members of different ethnic groups that have contributed to bird watching or ornithology."

"Have magazines like Audubon show ethnic groups and have articles that address their experience."

"Make speakers and bird walk guides available to community organizations. Invite these organizations to special programs designed for families."

"Use local newspapers and newsletters, radio and TV programs focused on their communities, and Internet sites. Place articles on birding for families, nature and health, nature and stress relief. Offer interviews. Create Web content or create a new Web site devoted to people of color in birding or people of color with interest in nature and ecology and conservation."

"Educational outreach should focus on what is available through the state park system."

There is a need for greater media awareness. If the media delivers the message that birding is for everyone, the industry will follow. The North American Bird Conservation Initiative, Partners in Flight, various "all-bird" conservation initiatives, the American Birding Association, National Audubon Society, and retail outlets such as Wild Birds Unlimited, Wild Bird Centers, and BirdWatch America can get together to deliver this message to local, regional, and national news media.

Anyone who hears this message must be welcomed and learn how they can benefit. What does this value look like? The collective energies and minds at the forefront of the bird watching, nature, and outdoor recreation industry are needed to build the message. Our vision should be to encourage interest in the outdoors, nature, and birds among people who have not yet had the opportunity to experience the joy and wonder of the environment that surrounds them. Some of these people will want to serve as an advocate for conservation of our natural resources.

Role Models and Mentors

Mentors are those who help us achieve our goals by having done what we aspire to do. The influence of role models is made that much easier from the many ways in which society communicates.

One of the twelve respondents had this to say about role models: "mentoring activities and role models are needed. In almost all aspects of birding and nature study, minorities have few if any role models to initiate their curiosity."

During one of the initial debates on minorities in bird watching that appeared in *Birding* magazine, the topic of role models was brought up. Lamar Gore at Back Bay National Wildlife Refuge stated, "I have to say that certain things are just not directed to Blacks, and I mean from childhood on up. The market has to make a conscious decision to seek out and court other groups. The interest can be aroused; I've seen it and caused it myself. A change in advertising and possible programs scheduled in the right areas, along with some support from Blacks who back this effort, can change everything." One of the 322 respondents to the first questionnaire observed, :...the insufficient number of role models is 'the most important factor' that would explain the relative absence of African Americans among birdwatchers." While there is no way to prove this statement as true, I would argue that it is an astute observation and explains some if not most of the absence of African Americans (and other minorities) from the ranks of birdwatchers.

Another respondent commented, "Tiger Woods and Jackie Robinson have shown the importance of a role model to the goal of increasing participation rates of diverse peoples in sports activities. I believe the same concept applies to bird watching."

There is always a team surrounding role models and mentors that enable them to rise to the level of performance that others respect and admire. Within the birding community, there already are potential role models and mentors for African Americans, Asians, Hispanics, and Native Americans. Their current achievements reflect the potential in them to become leaders in their field. However, they need support from their fellow birdwatchers, the media, and the bird-watching industry before they can become recognized as a bona fide role model or mentor. An effective outreach and recruitment program would highlight and promote the accomplishments and current activities of these individuals so others may be encouraged to follow them. In order to reach non-traditional bird-watching prospects, the effective use of role models and mentors is absolutely critical.

Most of us who study birds can identify with the analogy that birding is like catching a disease. Once you have it, it takes over your life. The enriching experience that birding offers to everyone who partakes even for a brief moment can create memories to last a lifetime.

An outreach and recruitment program must be the product of a collective set of minds working toward a common goal. There is always the risk that if a strategy is put forth in the absence of input from other influential people, then the whole effort may be shelved and delay the start of this important work.

The bird-watching industry needs to move forward with the creation and dissemination of the birding and nature message, and reach out to non-traditional audiences. Additional research needs to be done that is statistically significant and scientifically defendable to help propel the urgency and credibility behind this work. Any new information collected from further research should be used to correct any actions taken to reach non-traditional audiences.

To get started, all that is necessary is to review the information in these pages from minorities who already are birdwatchers and students of nature. Their voices should be considered a loud one, and their thoughts and recommendations receive the diligence that they deserve. I encourage others to join in what I have started and shape the future of birding and environmental conservation. The innovation that results from many people sharing ideas, concepts, and possible solutions is always better than the same product created by just one person.

Chapter 9

The Interviews

WHILE DOING RESEARCH for this book, I conducted interviews with active birders of various ethnic minority backgrounds. The purpose was to corroborate the results from the surveys and provide insight about the role minorities can play in outdoor recreation activities, especially bird watching. These interviews are a testament to the power that outreach and recruitment efforts could have if implemented widely and consistently. As you read the interviews, think about how you can use the information to spread the word that "birding is for everyone."

The following interviews with Sam Cuenca, Les Chibana, Keith Russell, and Carlotta Hargrove and her Fairchild Warblers, Gabino Garcia and LaToya Mabry, were conducted in the spring and summer of 2005.

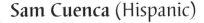

Sam Cuenca (Hispanic)

After obtaining his bachelor's degree from Humboldt State University in 1986, Sam began work as a biologist with the USDA Forest Service. Presently he is District Wildlife Biologist on the Scott / Salmon River Ranger District of the Klamath National Forest in Northern California. Much of his time at the Forest is spent addressing Threatened, Endangered, and Sensitive species issues. He coordinates the monitoring of avian and herpeto-logical species, which includes running of a bird monitoring station on the Klamath River and working with a newly described species of salamander, the genus *Plethodon* . Sam is also involved with conduct-ing conservation education-related activities with schools throughout the area. Outside of work he and his son explore many of the beauti-ful areas near their home in Siskiyou County.

What began your interest in bird watching?

My maternal grandmother had an enthusiastic interest in birds. She grew up in the mountains of the southern Sierra Madre, where she learned an appreciation of the natural world. She brought that appre-ciation with her when she moved to the United States and passed this on to her grandchildren. I spent much of my childhood camping, fish-ing, and hiking with my family in the Santa Cruz Mountains and Sierra Nevada. I have very early childhood memories watching birds at back-yard bird feeders with my family. I try to pass this interest to my son.

Describe how you first got involved in bird watching

My parents fostered my grandmother's enthusiasm by taking my sister and me on outdoor-related adventures. A high school biology teach-er recognized my interests and recommended me for my first summer job, working in natural resources. I worked nine seasons as an employee of Olympic National Park in western Washington. There I monitored

Spotted Owls, and surveyed Bald Eagle roost areas and pelagic birds in Puget Sound. During that time, I began pursuing my bachelor's degree in Wildlife Management at Humboldt State University (HSU).

At HSU, I had the honor of taking classes from Dr. Stan Harris. His courses formally introduced me to the science and passion of bird watching. I hold Dr. Harris in very high regard and thank him for sharing his knowledge.

During the summer of 1986, while working for California Department of Fish and Game, I met David Gaines in the town of Lee Vining. David became a good friend in the short time I knew him. He was an expert birder and author of field guides to the eastern Sierras. David's achievements included his instrumental role in the "Save the Mono Lake" efforts. David was an inspiration and I enjoyed birding with him.

As a wildlife biologist with the U.S Forest Service, bird monitoring is an important part of my job. I run a bird banding station on the Klamath River and monitor many avian Threatened, Endangered, and Sensitive Species, and lead bird-watching field trips for youth and local interest groups. I have been involved with many Christmas Bird Counts and events related to International Migratory Bird Day. In 2001, I had an opportunity to assist with coffee plantation bird monitoring in El Ocote Reserve in Chiapas, Mexico.

More recently as a wildlife biologist for the Klamath National Forest I have had many opportunities to learn from many extremely talented birders in my area. These include John Alexander, Bill Maynard, Joey Russell, Bob Claypole, and Ray Eckstrom.

Should more of the general public participate in bird watching, the study of nature, and the outdoors?

Many young people representing urban life of America are getting further removed from nature and the outdoors. This is influenced by cyber-technology. Though computers are integral to the advancement of education, an understanding and appreciation of nature is a perspective that must not be lost. Bird watching can be a key to an appreciation because of its accessibility and low cost, and takes place in many urban as well as rural settings. All one needs is a pair of binoculars, a bird book, and enthusiasm. It is also important that natural resource professionals share our knowledge and experience to encourage interest in the outdoors for young people.

Should more of your racial or ethnic group participate in bird watching, the study of nature, and the outdoors?

The appreciation of birds and nature is not based on ethnicity. That being said, I have often wondered if there is an aspect of bird watching tied to Hispanics with origins in Central and South America. My ancestors traveled across Mexico to establish a new life in the United States. The drive to find education, employment, and security, and reunite family inspired this epic journey. This is not much different from the challenge migratory birds make each year. As Hispanics, we should have a particular appreciation for the travels that birds have made.

What actions would you recommend to increase interest and participation in bird watching and the outdoors among people of color?

The Partners In Flight Program provides a private, state, and federal support to continue outreach and education to the public, including Asians, Blacks, Native Americans, and Hispanic peoples.

International Migratory Bird Day also provides a catalyst for outreach. More emphasis could be spent on specific outreach to urban and inner-city awareness.

Science courses taught at public schools should incorporate aspects of bird watching, gardening with natives, importance of shade-grown coffee, and habitat restoration, specifically to minority audiences. This includes increasing opportunities for field trips during the school year and re-establishment of recruitment summer internship programs (Student Conservation Association, California Conservation Corps, Youth Conservation Corps, and AmeriCorps).

Author's Note: Sam Cuenca has been a friend of mine for over a decade, and I was excited about including his story. The remembrance of his grandmother is especially poignant. Sam told me these were some of the fondest memories he had as a child.

I also asked Sam what it felt like to lead bird-watching field trips for local youth groups. He said he looks for those one or two people he connects with, and there is usually at least one at each presentation he gives. This connection is what Sam really strives for, because once this is established, he can pass his enthusiasm on to someone else. The success gives him incentive to continue his efforts. He knows his efforts are worthwhile when a boy or girl comes up to him in town on a later date and says, "You're the bird guy!"

However, what touched me most was Sam's analogy between bird migration and the immigration of his ancestors from Mexico into the United States. Sam saw this analogy as an opportunity for Hispanics to see the wonder of bird migration in terms of their own ancestry.

Les Chibana (Asian American)

Les Chibana has led birding trips in Alaska, Hawaii (including the Midway Atoll), Southeast Arizona, and California (including Monterey Bay pelagic trips). In the San Francisco Bay Area, he teaches an intermediate / advanced birding class for the City of Palo Alto and has a bird guiding business, BirdNUTZ. He banded land birds with the San Francisco Bay Bird Observatory for a number of years, focusing on migrant perching birds. He is an avid bird photographer and does freelance graphic design when not out looking for birds.

What began your interest in bird watching?

I helped a friend hand-raise a Red-crested Cardinal in Hawaii, getting an in-hand experience with a wild bird. I also helped release it back into the wild.

Describe how you first got involved in bird watching

I went on a hike in the Santa Cruz Mountains with the San Jose State University campus chapter of the Sierra Club. One of the leaders pointed out a Rufous-sided Towhee. That struck me as one of those ridiculous names the geeks interested in birds would pronounce, like "Yellow-bellied Sapsucker." My impression of birdwatchers was influenced by television. I thought they were like Nancy Culp's character in the *Beverly Hillbillies*, John McGavin in a movie that I've forgotten, or that arrogant birdwatcher / ornithologist woman in Alfred Hitchcock's *The Birds*. Birdwatchers were socially awkward people who wore safari jackets and pith helmets. I was delighted when I found out that field guides existed. Since I knew no other birders nor owned a pair of binoculars, my interest lay inactive until I was gainfully employed. I purchased a pair of binoculars and asked a close friend to go out looking for birds with me.

I didn't know about the local Audubon Chapters or other birders. I stopped at interesting places and searched for birds, taking what pictures I could without a telephoto lens. I was established in a job in Palo Alto, when my future wife told me about a bird-watching class offered at the adult education school. We took the beginning and intermediate level classes taught by Jim Rosso, and tried to learn as much about birding as possible. After five years of enjoying the classes and being introduced to the greater birding community, I took over the classes because Jim moved from the area. I had volunteered to band birds at Coyote Creek Riparian Station (now field station with San Francisco Bay Bird Observatory) three years prior to taking over the classes, and begun to take more bird photos, now with a telephoto lens. I led two birding trips to Hawaii for Cheeseman's Ecology Safaris, then three trips to Alaska with Sierra Club Outings.

Should more of the general public participate in bird watching, the study of nature, and the outdoors?

Everyone needs a grasp of the interrelatedness of the elements of our environment, and how our behavior impacts our environment. We need to understand the value of indicator species, and that the seeming vastness of nature is not endless and indestructible. Birding is a great way for people to become interested in wildlife and their habitats and begin to understand these connections.

Should more of your racial or ethnic group participate in bird watching, the study of nature, and the outdoors?

Asian people are expected to become one of the most numerous people on the earth. It is extremely important that this population have an awareness of our ecosystem. They have the potential to consume enough resources to make a significant impact.

What actions would you recommend to increase interest and participation in bird watching and the outdoors among people of color?

I teach birding classes, and have seen how people's interest and awareness of the environment and wildlife issues increase with their participation. Offering classes in birding can be a way to reach some ethnic groups. However, this may not be enough. The right cultural appeal needs to be identified in order to make the class appealing to different ethnic groups.

The idea of birding as stress reduction may appeal to some people, but this may only be for those who can afford the time and basic gear. While they are enjoying the stress reduction, birding will also introduce them to an appreciation of wildlife.

Author's Note: I met Les Chibana at several birding festivals and trade shows, and was very impressed by his calm personality and friendliness. During the interview, I learned how successful Les has been at mentoring others through the birding classes he teaches. Some of his students have now gone on to become teachers themselves.

Les has that rare mix of natural confidence and honest modesty about his abilities. His enthusiasm for studying birds has propelled him forward and allowed him to succeed in his endeavors.

Soon after he took an interest in birds and birding, Les told me, other birders would point out birds to him, causing him to think just how many other birds there were out there that he was missing. This is as close as anyone has ever come to describing the feelings that I experienced when I first started.

During our interview, Les agreed that money is not a limitation or barrier preventing someone from studying birds, especially if used to relieve stress or simply to relax.

Les also told me a fascinating story of the time he was at a gas station getting his car fixed by a Chinese mechanic. He told the mechanic he was a birder who took other people bird watching. The mechanic was surprised by this and said he expected Les never had Chinese clients because "Chinese are not interested in nature." I have heard similar stories told about and by African Americans. One day Les and I will hear people of Asian descent casually state, "Chinese *are* interested in nature."

I asked Les whether he thought it would be possible to introduce birding to non-traditional audiences. No obstacle is too large to overcome, he said.

Keith Russell (African American)

Keith Russell was born in 1956 in Augusta, Georgia, but raised in Philadelphia, Pennsylvania. He is the oldest of seven children and he attended Philadelphia public schools, then completed his high school education at the Germantown Friends School. He became interested in birds at the age of seven and his passion for birds led him to pursue biology as a major in college. In 1977, he graduated from Cornell University with a degree in biology and in 1981 he received a Master of Science in zoology from Clemson University. He worked for the Academy of Natural Sciences of Philadelphia from 1982 to 2003, first as collection manager for the Academy's exhibits department, then as assistant editor for *Birds of North America*, a publication produced by the Academy's ornithology department. He is currently a biologist for the National Audubon Society's Important Bird Area program. In addition to ornithology his interests include classical music, art, classic films, and weightlifting.

What began your interest in bird watching?

I remember giving a report on birds in the third grade. There was a request to do a verbal report and I chose birds because I liked them. Both of my parents were well educated and employed in professional jobs, and the atmosphere in our home allowed children to pursue any interest that might catch their attention. Children who lack a supporting influence may develop an interest in something like bird watching, but it quickly wanes without the kind of support I had.

Describe how you first got involved in bird watching

My interest in birds did not come from my parents, but they supported me by buying binoculars and books for my use, and also by taking me to the library.

I was really interested in art and drawing birds and I used to go to the Academy of Natural Sciences and draw the birds on display. While doing this, I got to know the naturalists that worked there, one of whom was Stephen Harty, who became my mentor. Stephen was also in charge of the field trip program at the Academy.

My parents found people who were also interested in birds and introduced them to me. One of these individuals was Joseph Cadberry, a teacher and Quaker who taught science at a Germantown school in Philadelphia. He eventually became another important mentor of mine. I talked every week with Mr. Cadberry and he patiently listened to my reports of my bird sightings, even when I erred in the identification.

My parents enrolled all seven of us into the Germantown high school where Mr. Cadberry taught science. There were lots of students who were interested in birds and birding, and a very accepting atmosphere. Kids did not get teased for wanting to study birds.

I joined the Delaware Valley Ornithological Club in 1973, when I was seventeen. This also provided support.

Should more of the general public participate in bird watching, the study of nature, and the outdoors?

Yes, it makes you a better and more well-rounded person. There are a lot of miracles in nature that benefit us if we have had the opportunity to experience them. In addition, there are political opinions and decisions to be made each day and we need to be informed when we make such decisions or when we cast our vote. Here is one example: what products do you use on your lawn or backyard? You don't want to use products that could kill birds, right? We can only make such a decision if we have the awareness to know this is an issue.

From a spiritual perspective, to be in tune with nature and enjoy its beauty and wonder is another reason why we should know more.

Should more of your racial or ethnic group participate in bird watching, the study of nature, and the outdoors?

There are important reasons why our participation is not higher than it is. Some of these are historical, and others are very complicated.

Yet I still believe it is important for us to know more about nature and the outdoors.

What actions would you recommend to increase interest and participation in bird watching and the outdoors among people of color?

Exposure is quite important. Many kids in large cities don't go anywhere and don't get to see the things we have seen in nature. Exposure can happen with television, but must be followed up by seeing the real thing. Increased exposure is the foundation for any interest, be it birding or other pursuits.

There needs to be support and mentoring, people you can work with and learn from, or participate in activities with. This is similar to an apprenticeship where you learn from someone who has already done what you would like to do. Mentoring can take many different forms.

Role models are needed. Although I was raised in a manner that did not make it necessary to see Black role models before taking an interest in something, role models can have a strong influence on young people. Many people are more comfortable doing something for the first time if they see others already active in that field, whatever it may be.

Author's Notes: Keith Russell was one of the people who responded to the questionnaire I used during the first phase of my investigation. A friend of mine told me about the work Keith Russell was doing on the *Birds of North America* project. While I did not usually talk to all those who responded to the questionnaire, I called Keith and discussed my work with him. He was very interested, and encouraged me to keep him updated on my progress.

Until I talked to Keith I could think of no better way to say why it is important that we should be interested in nature and the outdoors, let alone birds. However, Keith reminded me that we make decisions every day, and many affect the earth and environment, though at varying scales. Keith's message is simple: we make better decisions if we are more informed, and education and awareness can be obtained from studying nature and developing a passion for the outdoors. Birding is one avenue by which we can achieve this.

Keith also told me the importance of a person or group of people who can provide supporting influence that can help maintain a person's interest. All too often, someone may take up an interest in birds or nature, only to have it wane because there is no supporting infrastructure to keep them engaged. Think of how wonderful it is to hear about young inner city or minority children who have developed an interest in the outdoors on their own. Now, think of how sad it is when this burning interest flickers out and dies a few days, weeks, or months later because no one was available to support them. Although it is important to provide opportunities for young people to be exposed to nature, birding, and enjoying the outdoors; support from schools, parents, role models, and mentors is the most important cog in the machine, even more important than exposure.

Carlotta Hargrove
(African American)

Carlotta Hargrove was born in Cincinnati, Ohio, and moved to Texas in 1985, where she started bird watching in earnest. She opened the Youth With High Potential Program at the Fairchild Park and Tennis Center in San Antonio, where children ages six to seventeen learned tennis, birding, tae kwan do, golf, gardening, and archery. She remains active at the center.

What began your interest in bird watching?

I have always enjoyed bird watching, even from when I was a child. At that time I just watched birds, without the idea of trying to identify what they were. I did not become involved in bird watching until I moved to Texas. Thomas Cleaver, a friend and neighbor, wanted to get involved in bird watching and we started together.

Describe how you first got involved in bird watching

Bird watching as a hobby sort of evolved. We purchased binoculars and birding books and started identifying the birds we saw in our neighborhood. It was amazing the colors that could be seen through binoculars not visible to the naked eye. To go bird watching and identify as many birds as possible became a challenge. In the beginning, we took a long time to identify even a couple of birds, but we became more proficient as time went on.

Later, we started an after-school and summer enrichment program for at-risk youth, and introduced bird watching as a component of the program. At first the youth involved in the program were not interested; however, soon many of them began to enjoy it and ask to go bird watching. We went bird watching with them wherever we would travel. They competed in the National Junior Tae Kwon Do Olympics in Florida and Minnesota, and we stopped along the way to bird watch.

While in Florida, the youth had an opportunity to bird watch in the Everglades. Birding provided them with an opportunity to travel and explore locations many would not have imagined possible.

Should more of your racial or ethnic group participate in bird watching, the study of nature, and the outdoors?

I run an after-school and summer enrichment program for at-risk, multicultural youth, predominantly African American and Hispanic. When Thomas Cleaver and I began the program, most of the kids had never been camping or hiking, or even heard of bird watching. Most of them began bird watching under duress. We gave them no choice in the matter. However, they learned to enjoy birding and some became really great at it. We would be driving down a road and they'd scream out, "Stop, go back! I saw a bird in the field." They developed this game for road trips where they would take turns going through the birding books and describing birds. The first person to name the bird being described would have the opportunity to find another bird in the book for the others to identify.

The kids in our program love the study of nature and the outdoors in general. They are constantly asking when we are going camping again. Usually we have several big campouts per year, and try to do at least one every season, with our big campout occurring at the end of the summer. Last year we went to Tyler State Park and it was absolutely wonderful. When we took the kids in the program camping, the ones who presented us with the worst behavior seemed to be at peace in nature. That is not to say that there were no problems at the campsite, but they were considerably less in severity and duration. The youth enjoyed putting up tents, cooking meals, exploring the flora and fauna, and listening to and sometimes being afraid of the sounds of the night.

The other day, some of the kids were reminiscing about past camping trips. They told tales about raccoons raiding the campsite, walking to the restrooms at night and how afraid they were, and the first time putting a worm on the end of a hook to go fishing. One night they were caught in a thunderstorm and their tent collapsed, and they slept in the van until next morning. The stories went on. Since we can't take all the kids camping at the same time, the trips are great rewards for good behavior.

Bird watching and the study of nature can also be relaxing. It is a perfect way to unwind and leave the pressures of everyday life behind. There is something special about the sound of leaves rustling in the breeze as trees sway overhead, sunlight as it filters through branches and leaves and creates patterns below, or the sound of nature as you awake in the morning or as you fall asleep at night in your tent. We have taken the kids to beaches in Galveston and Corpus Christi and the same can be said of the sound of waves crashing against the shore, and the reflections of nature in the water. I have found that the outdoors truly has a magical and calming effect upon most kids.

It is a great way for families and friends to spend quality time together. Recently I met some family members in Hawaii for vacation. While there, my husband, daughter (age 24), two sons (ages 29 and 26), my two-year-old grandson, my sister, her husband and their two children, and niece climbed Diamond Head together. The next day my husband, children, grandson, and brother-in-law climbed to Manoa Falls, which is a rainforest. The weather had been beautiful the whole time we were in Hawaii, but the day we decided to climb to Manoa Falls it rained. We waited for a while hoping the rain would cease, but then decided to climb anyway. We covered ourselves with towels, made ponchos from garbage bags, and set out on our journey. My son carried his two-year-old on his shoulders most of the way to the waterfall and back down again. It was wonderful, a great family bonding experience. The highlights of our vacation were almost all nature related.

Even though the trip was to Hawaii, it doesn't have to involve some faraway, exotic location. There are state parks and national parks and wildlife refuges all around, and the beauty of nature is everywhere. The key is taking the time to enjoy it, both in solitude and in the company of family and friends. Nature has a way of bringing people together. The appreciation of nature and its beauty is a great common denominator.

What actions would you recommend to increase interest and participation in bird watching and the outdoors among people of color?

We need to involve youth in bird watching and the study of nature and the outdoors. If they can learn to appreciate and enjoy these activities when young, chances are they will continue into their adult lives and pass along that appreciation to their children.

Also important is for youth groups to involve minorities and at-risk youth who might not have an opportunity to become involved in these activities. We have found this has a profound effect on kids' behavior and their self-esteem as they explore the natural world and its many facets.

Schools need to encourage the appreciation of nature and nature-related activities. Bird watching, gardening, study of native plants and animals, hiking, and camping, are pursuits that bring endless hours of enjoyment for any individual.

Not only do our youth need to be educated about the enjoyment of the outdoors, they should also know there are fantastic jobs and careers related to plants, animals, nature, and our natural environment. For the child fascinated with birds, snakes, or wildlife and nature in general, this can be a potential career path.

Author's Notes: Meeting Carlotta Hargrove and Thomas Cleaver, Jr., was the most fortunate thing to happen as a result of conducting my research. Their work has touched me in so many ways that any attempt to describe it in words would pale by comparison.

Although I never personally met them, I talked with Thomas and we exchanged several emails before his untimely death. In addition, I have had numerous conversations and correspondence with Carlotta while preparing this book. Their story has been the inspiration to finish this project.

During a recent telephone interview with Carlotta, I asked her how she got her youth program started. Originally it was run during two afternoons each week after school, with the expenses for the program coming out of Carlotta's pocket. Then the city pitched in with a part-time salary. Word of mouth had more kids joining the program. Her goal was to help these kids become successful in their lives, no matter their surroundings. She started with tennis to attract the kids, and bird watching was added later. Birding was something she and Thomas enjoyed as a hobby, and they involved the kids in what they did as adults.

At first the kids thought she and Thomas were crazy. Imagine having two adults tell you, "Here is a pair of binoculars and a bird book. This is where we are going and the birds we are looking for." Although members of the youth program admit they were "forced" into bird watching, the experience opened their eyes and some of these kids became truly skilled birders.

I asked Carlotta how she has grown as an individual from the experience of running the youth program. The pride and spirit in her answer was unmistakable. She has seen noticeable changes in the children she works with. Moreover, the kids recognized that she and Thomas cared for them, in effect making the Youth with High Potential program their "home away from home." Thomas and Carlotta were like the kids' surrogate mom and dad. An experience like that is bound to result in tremendous personal growth. Carlotta believes she has become more tolerant and understanding as a result.

To know that their program is successful is not enough. The work Carlotta continues to do involves both the kids and the parents of those kids. One parent asked Carlotta, "How can I teach my daughter what to do when I don't know myself?" Birding is an aspect of this. These kids come from a "have not" versus a "have" environment, which is where most birders come from. Through her work, one child at a time, Carlotta is changing that.

Gabino Garcia (Hispanic) and Latoya Mabry (African American) of the Fairchild Warblers

LaToya Mabray and Gabino Garcia of San Antonio, Texas, joined the Youth With High Potential Program in 1996 and 1997. Their primary interests include birds, tennis, and tae kwon do karate (both of them are black belts). They participated in the Great Texas Coastal Birding Classic, and represented the winning team of the Fairchild Warblers.

What began your interest in bird watching?

LaToya Mabry: Thomas Cleaver and Carlotta Hargrove introduced me to birding and I wanted to learn more.

Gabino Garcia: We were forced into bird watching by coming to Fairchild Park and Tennis Center. They ran a program named "Youth with High Potential." Bird watching was one of the activities included. If we wanted to be a part of the program, we had to participate.

Describe how you first got involved in bird watching

Mabry: Thomas and Carlotta took a group of us bird watching, and I recorded as well as found birds. In the beginning I wasn't really good at naming the birds. A year later I was more interested and wanted to learn the names. I looked them up in the field guide and became familiar with how the birds looked and began to appreciate the beauty of the birds and their different colors and distinguishing marks.

The excitement of seeing a new bird was amazing. Once we became good at it we entered the Great Texas Coastal Birding Classic. Being able to go to different places and see different birds made me enjoy birding even more.

Garcia: We started going to San Antonio Audubon Society meetings and entered the Great Texas Coastal Birding Classic. I liked it because it was competitive. We won third place two years in a row and first place two years in a row. I found that I was really good at finding and identifying birds. Also, the hobby kept me out of trouble. I had a small pair of binoculars I loved and when I was home and bored, I'd go outside and look for birds. Sometimes I would call Thomas or Carlotta and describe a bird I could not find in the book and they would help me identify it. I started spending more time outside. My favorite bird was the Cedar Waxwing and a flock of them came to my house.

Should more of your racial or ethnic group participate in bird watching, the study of nature, and the outdoors?

Mabry: Bird watching and being interested in nature activities give you the chance to leave your problems for a while and focus on something different. It keeps you from being on the street, or selling or using drugs, and calms you down. Nature teaches you things such as science that will help in school. I used to be uninterested in science and was not good at it. Going birding and identifying habitats made science more interesting and easier to understand.

Garcia: The main reason for birding is that it's fun. Nature activities, such as bird watching, camping, and fishing, are very enjoyable. The outdoors and woods are peaceful. It is also educational. Another reason is that nature helps keep kids busy and out of trouble.

What actions would you recommend to increase interest and participation in bird watching and the outdoors among people of color?

Mabry: One way would be through science classes in school. Before I met Thomas and Carlotta, I knew nothing about bird watching. They have everything else in school except bird watching and outdoor activities, such as camping and nature appreciation. Teaching these activities in school would get more kids interested in doing them on their own.

Getting kids involved in competitions such as the Great Texas Coastal Birding Classic is another way to increase interest in bird watching. These competitions are a lot of fun and give inner city kids a chance to see the countryside and different birds.

Membership in organizations, like the San Antonio Audubon Society and bird-watching clubs, is important. They go on many outings for bird watching and studying nature, and can teach you how to improve your birding skills.

Garcia: Having more activities such as the Great Texas Coastal Birding Classic would increase interest in bird watching.

I'd like to see television commercials featuring minorities promoting bird watching and other outdoor activities and programs. Commercials are successful in convincing people to purchase a variety of products. Why not use them to promote nature activities?

Local bird-watching associations can get minority kids involved in bird watching and outdoor programs by going into schools and talking about some of the activities and how much fun they can be. Kids love binoculars and just showing how to use them is a great way to introduce bird watching.

Chapter 10

The Challenge—
Are You Up For It?

THE THANKSGIVING HOLIDAYS of November 2005 finds me writing this last chapter of *Birding for Everyone*. My journey began autumn 1999 in a Kernville, California, hotel room, contemplating why so many people on meeting me for the first time exclaimed, "I've never met a Black birdwatcher before." It was then I decided to write *Birding for Everyone*. Six years later the journey has come to a fruitful and memorable end. Yet this is really the beginning for what must come next.

In June 2005, KESQ Channel 3 in Palm Springs, California, reported the Santa Clara Valley Chapter of the National Audubon Society was reaching out to Hispanics in an attempt to "expand beyond its predominantly white membership." The Chapter did this by hosting a book-signing event for Kenn Kaufman, to recognize his *Guia de Campo* field guide to the birds of North America, the first such guide entirely in Spanish.

Associated Press writer Pauline Jelinek reported on June 9, 2005 that Hispanics are the fastest-growing minority in the United States, representing one-seventh of all people in the US. This increase is attributable to both immigration and higher birth rates. Moreover, while a "far greater percentage of whites than Hispanics is 65 [years of age] or older, the opposite is true of those under 18." According to the Census Bureau statistics cited by Jelinek, the size of the Hispanic population rose in nearly every state during the course of the 1990s, and similar trends were also seen among Asian population statistics.

Associated Press writer Michael Hill reported on August 26, 2005 that minorities avoid wilderness activities. In his article, Bunyan Bryant, director of the University of Michigan's Environmental Justice Initiative, is quoted as saying that he has seen the same thing while camping on the shores of Lake Huron over the past several decades: "green trees, blue skies, and white people." Reporter Hill wrote that wilderness advocates and administrators are currently reaching out to Blacks, Hispanics, and Asians in an attempt to correct the lack of ethnic and racial diversity in outdoor areas and activities such as hiking, camping, mountain biking, boating, and others. Cultural factors cannot be ignored, as evidenced by Marta Maldonado of Iowa State University's sociology department, who believes that the concept of wilderness is "a western European idea, not one necessarily shared by minority groups." Yet public land advocates are concerned about the growing minority constituency who will weigh in on land use policies.

Finally, in the fall of 2005, Audrey Peterman published an article called "Continental Divide" in *National Parks* magazine. She talks about her first foray into the National Park system in 1995 (visiting 14 National Parks and encompassing 12,000 miles) during which time she saw only two other Black people in the parks. She cites a focus group report from the National Park Service in which African Americans said they felt as though national parks did not relate to them. Following her journey in 1995, Audrey Peterman and husband Frank began publishing a newsletter, *Pickup & Go!*, the purpose of which is "to get the word out and to promote the relevance of the parks to all Americans." Peterman reports that progress on these issues remains slow, and the Park Service continues to report that attracting diverse visitors and employees is a goal yet to be achieved. She ends her article with an observation and an anecdote:

> "*The sterling legacy of a National Park System cannot be sustained if the fastest-growing demographic groups have no connection with them. Friends living within 30 minutes of [the Florida] Everglades, who had never visited before, became hooked once we took them to the park, and testified in support of protecting it when the need arose.*"

So what do we do? This book has been prepared for the mainstream birder who recognizes the need for greater diversity among birders and outdoor recreationists; the bird-watching industry; and people of color who may be contemplating expanding (or initiating) their study of nature and the outdoors, perhaps through birds. Each of these audiences has a unique challenge before them. As we look at the possible solutions to be woven into an outreach and recruitment strategy, the response from each of these three audiences will be distinctly different. These different responses must also be united.

One of the most enjoyable experiences I had while writing this book was interviewing Gabino Garcia and LaToya Mabry. I hope I have touched them in some way and given them the gift of interest in nature Ted Lee Eubanks talks about. This is a gift I am sure they had already received from their experiences with Thomas Cleaver, Jr. and Carlotta Hargrove, but it is also a gift that cannot be given often enough. How they mold the interest into recreational pursuits remains to be seen, but my bet is the future is pretty bright for them and the conservation issues they will come in contact with over their lives.

I challenge all who have read this book to begin a dialogue with at least three other people on what the next steps should be. The road to progress will not be easy, but the opportunity for major improvement exists.

If you are a person of color thinking of birding or making visits to a national forest or park, I challenge you to take that first step. Remember, you do not need permission to do this.

If you are a mainstream birder and / or member of the bird-watching industry, join forces with one another to investigate how the findings and recommendations provided in this book can be used to the best advantage to ensure our precious natural resources remain available for generations to come. Shared vision and united persistence are needed to achieve the results necessary (and realistically achievable) to bridge this divide in conservation. My purpose in inviting two colleagues, Paul Baicich and Ted Lee Eubanks, to comment on my findings leads by example: their insights, combined with mine, create a synergy I could not have achieved on my own. As conservationists, we must repeat this process on an increasingly larger scale.

The history of our country is filled with examples of times when conservation efforts came too little and too late. The Passenger Pigeon, the Ivory-billed Woodpecker, and the Dusky Seaside Sparrow are just birds that come to mind. *Birding for Everyone* is not about the endangerment of a particular species or habitat; it is about the endangerment of conservation itself. We still have time to initiate the necessary changes. However, without action, in another twenty five to fifty years, it may be too late.

In late July 2005, on my last day before retiring from a twenty five-year career with the federal service, a colleague of mine gave me a print out from an Internet page belonging to the Sierra Club. An anonymous teacher at George Washington Elementary school in Philadelphia is quoted as saying: "The rule of the street is tough on children. Getting away from the violence and dirt of the city is the only way I can do the extra things, the important things, with the children. I can teach and develop minds in a classroom but I can only work on the spirit, soul, and character in the woods." I can think of no better example that should inspire how we engage our youth over the coming decades.

The aim of *Birding for Everyone* is to not change people or their cultures. I want to simply make them more aware. Birding *IS* for everyone. Is it for you?

Comments by Ted Lee Eubanks

As President of FERMATA, Inc., Ted Lee Eubanks is involved in studying and promoting experiential tourism as a sustainable economic approach for communities. He currently resides in Austin, Texas.

Socialization is a well-studied process in heritage outdoor recreations such as hunting and fishing. Yet for birding and wildlife viewing this process is less well understood. To consider the implications of John Robinson's findings we must first explore precisely how one becomes a birder.

Perhaps a place to start is by defining birding. Of the 70 million birders reported in the National Survey on Recreation and the Environment (NSRE), how many identify with the label "birder"? In truth, most are involved with residential birding and do not consider themselves to be part of a larger recreational culture. These "birders" limit their involvement to bird feeders, gardening, martin houses, and other backyard activities. A far smaller minority actually bird away from the home; in other words, are recreational birders.

Rather than obsessing over the lack of minority birders (birding defined in its traditional sense) I suggest expanding birding to include anyone who finds their way to nature through birds. The challenge presented by John Robinson is more focused on how to bring more minority participants into *recreational* birding. On a larger scale I wonder about the barriers to minority populations finding both the resource (birds) and the recreation (birding) at any level of commitment and involvement.

Certainly being a recreational birder demands more than purchasing binoculars and a field guide. At a basic social level birding is attitudinal, and being a birder involves self-perception as well as a willingness to be part of the larger birding culture. Birding socialization is not an isolated process, and it depends on an extensive social system of initiators, mentors, and associates. Lifelong participation in birding is critically linked to both a personal as well as a cultural identification.

Yet what if within a defined population (geographic, ethnic, or racial) no such recreational culture and support system exists? What if there are no cohorts who are self-identified recreationists (birders or hunters, for example)? What if there is no larger recreational culture within the population? What if there are no mentors? What if there are no initiators? What if there are no friends to join in the recreation? I suppose a few might eventually wend their way to the recreation, but the journey would be circuitous and difficult.

I believe this to be the most important of John Robinson's findings. Within certain populations in the United States (African American, Hispanic, Asian) there is no tradition of birding. Within these populations there is no culture of birding, and few cohorts who are self-identified birders. Socialization is an entirely random affair, depending on happenstance.

The final question is: What can anyone do about the lack of minority participation in birding, given the above? In the short term, I believe we can do very little. However, in the long term, increased minority participation will be linked to how successfully the recreation is assimilated into each population's social and cultural context. In South Texas we have seen how participation among Hispanics has increased as birding and wildlife viewing have become adopted as family activities. The involvement of school-age children in a variety of birding activities has fueled much of this growth.

The key is to bring birding to these minority populations rather than waiting for them to find birding. The traditional white birding structure (bird clubs, Christmas Bird Counts, monthly bird lectures) may itself be one of the barriers keeping minorities at bay. We should focus on developing new ways of helping non-traditional populations find their way to nature through birds, and we should worry less about how they might then mold that interest into a meaningful recreational pursuit. Give them ownership and we give ourselves a future.

Comments by Paul J. Baicich

Mr. Baicich helps coordinate the Swarovski Optik Birding Community for North America and the National Wildlife Refuge Association.

How do we take the inquiry John Robinson has initiated and put it into practice? His insights and findings need to find vehicles in which to explore and experiment.

The birding community is composed of the core businesses involved in the subculture (optics, backyard birding, tour companies), the festival network, the clubs, the bird observatories, the magazines (commercial and non-commercial), and the stewards of the birding hotspots (refuges, forests, parks). Today the community is in a position to make a real difference in appealing to minorities.

This effort will not be easy, because the results will not appear instantly or particularly impressive. The effort will experience some false starts and dead ends, but by building on what John Robinson has uncovered, we can proceed.

Before going into prescriptions, let me pursue two important points: image and mentors.

When publisher John H. Johnson died in early August 2005, he was lauded as one of the most influential African Americans of his time. He launched his career through the founding of *Ebony* and *Jet* magazines after WW II. These publications countered the stereotypical coverage of African Americans in America, and made them feel part of the fabric of society. In the late 1950s and through the 1960s, Johnson's publications, particularly *Ebony*, chronicled not only the events of the Civil Rights movement, but just as importantly, portrayed African Americans desiring a life in America that was "normal."

The image of African American life was transformed at these years, and Johnson played an important part. Shopping at major stores, buying homes, attending graduations, participating in family gatherings, and going on vacation could be aspirations shared by Black Americans as well as White. The photographs in *Ebony* of Blacks doing these things were a revelation to Americans of all races. The ads didn't hurt either. (Reportedly, Johnson sent an ad salesman to Detroit every week for ten years before the first auto manufacturer agreed to advertise in *Ebony*.)

The birding community should do likewise. The image of birding as a "normal" activity has increased in the past decade, but the image of the minority birder remains virtually nonexistent. Something must be done. We need to raise the image of birding and minority birding at the same time.

The first recommendation on image overlaps with mentors and role models. John Robinson makes a good case for the need to engender role models and teachers among minority birders. Simply put, we need more Thomas Cleavers and Carlotta Hargroves. We need them for the birding community as a whole, as well as for our minority efforts. Before the middle of the twentieth century, the nascent bird-watching community had an informal army of "imbuers," as characterized by Joseph Kastner in his incisive book, *A World of Watchers* (see bibliography). Often these were teachers, librarians, and people whose names were prefixed by "Miss." We desperately need this again, and not just to appeal to minorities.

With image and mentors in mind, let me make some suggestions, building on John Robinson's foundation.

Clubs

Local bird clubs, be they Audubon chapters, county clubs, or affiliates of state ornithological networks, have to break out of their self-imposed isolation. They are, in most cases, increasingly irrelevant to the growing population curious about birds, and certainly irrelevant to minority communities. Bird clubs are usually not newcomer-friendly to either Whites or Blacks. The clubs are often hierarchical and wed to a meeting-style contrived in the mid-twentieth century or earlier. They need to be more family-friendly, educational, and engaged in community events. If there is an opening in the local school curriculum for an aspect of bird study, the bird club should be the intervener of choice. The vibrant and creative clubs I have witnessed run regular birding classes based on seasonal learning opportunities, and not simply run through a routine of monthly meetings, field trips, and requisite annual dinner.

If these flaws are addressed, they may help clubs in general, but clubs need to make a special effort to reach minorities and minority families in their ongoing activities. This will be a slow process, but there is little alternative.

Bird Observatories

Bird observatories in the US have grown over the past few decades to where there are now about fifty in operation. Starting in the mid-1960s, some of the older ones (like Cape May Bird Observatory, Point Reyes Bird Observatory, Whitefish Point Bird

Observatory, and Manomet Bird Observatory (now Manomet
Center for Conservation Sciences) are familiar to most birders.
The growing observatories can be volunteer and visitor-friendly,
or more research-oriented, appearing distant to the uninitiated. They find their own best mode of operation. The ones with a
broad spectrum of programs, particularly introductory programs,
are best suited to be a point of intersection for our specific concerns here.

These active observatories are also ideal in making the connection between appreciating birds and saving them. Research and
monitoring may be an observatory's main purpose, but education
is the key driver for its public activities. Like a bird club that par-
ticipates in regular birding classes for the young and old novice,
the bird observatory is another place to connect with the minority community. The observatory and the club must make the initial effort to reach out to minorities, and not wait to be found by
the minority community.

Festivals

Birding and nature festivals emerge like mushrooms after a rain
only to disappear after a short time; others arise year after year.
Festivals require no prior commitment from the participants, are
highly family-friendly, and don't demand much time from those
attending. You can sample the goods at your own pace. Festivals
are ideally placed to introduce minorities, especially minority
families, to birds and birding, if the correct amount of prior work
is done to attract them in the first place.

The advantages of festivals — one-time, no-commitment, friendly, fun introductions to regional birds — are also a potential dis-
advantage. For those who want to continue to learn about birds
and birding after the festival, there must be an enduring way to
make that possible. Enter the engaged bird club or bird observatory, refuge and nature centers, or creative businesses.

Refuges and Nature Centers

Centers of birding are the portals through which the uninitiated passes. These are park nature centers, National Wildlife Refuge visitor centers (visited for a map or a rest stop before the obligatory loop-road circuit), or virtually any stop on the growing network of birding trails spreading across the country. Stewards of these portals must devise creative ways to make every visitor a valued guest and potential birder. Minority visitors should be made welcome with every amenity. Each encounter is a learning opportunity. It is not unrealistic to approach visitation, particularly from minorities, with an evangelical zeal.

Magazines

Here's where our *Ebony* parallel emerges. We need more discussion of bird watching undertaking a dialogue with minority America, and revealing pictures that reflect that future. Both commercial magazines (like *Bird Watcher's Digest*, *Wild Bird*, and *Birders' World*) and those connected to non-profits (like *Birding* and *Living Bird*) need to be active players in the quest to make our pastime "look more like America."

Optics Companies

The optics companies are becoming more occupied in understanding the needs of birders. Led first by Swarovski and Leica, companies like Nikon, Zeiss, Steiner, Brunton, and others are making real efforts to reach out to our needs and desires. They also need to help address correcting our imperfections. The minority gap is one such imperfection. The optics companies can start by understanding where we need to go and supporting that effort.

The Backyard Industry

The backyard birding industry — from bird feeder manufacturers and birdseed companies to franchise stores — should follow the developments in attracting minorities with an eye to creative business practices. It is not enough to sell feeders and seed to the same folks in the same communities. The industry needs to pitch entry-level backyard birding to minority communities. (Remember John Robinson's first quizzical encounter with a Downy Woodpecker on a feeder.) The stores are perfectly situated to answer those essential questions concerning backyard stewardship, first in Black middle class suburbia (for example, around Washington, DC and Atlanta, Georgia), and then elsewhere.

The Plans

Bird plans from the North American Waterfowl Management Plan, the U. S. Shorebird Conservation Plan, to Partners in Flight, are woefully inadequate in promoting bird appreciation. The plans often reflect a limited dialogue between biologists and managers, with the human dimension left out of the picture. The future of birds is not dependent on the right plan, but on a constituency committed to the survival of birds. That constituency cannot thrive without being a multicultural mosaic. Bird plans not only need to plan for on-the-ground conservation, they should also promote a vibrant and varied bird constituency.

We in the broad birding community are in an ideal position to make a real difference in appealing to minorities, but we have to choose to make that effort. Whether we make that collective choice remains to be seen. I hope we do.

Appendix A

Questionnaires

Questionnaire Used to Describe African Americans'
Level of Participation in Bird Watching

African American Birder Research Form

This survey is to sample African Americans only.

The two basic questions here are what percentage of African Americans are birdwatchers (which will be answered in the Participation Module) and what barriers prevent African Americans from participating in bird watching. We don't want to bias the sample pool only to those African Americans who have stated they have previously participated in bird watching. These questions should be asked of all African Americans.

Questions on the first page are asked of participants and every other non-participant.

- *Are you a member of a local birding club or other bird-watching organization?*

- *Are you a member of a national environmental group, such as the Audubon Society or the National Wildlife Federation?*

- *How many species of wild birds can you name?*
  ❑ 1–5   ❑ 6–10   ❑ 11–20   ❑ 21 or more

- *Do you feed birds with a bird feeder?*

- *How many times did you visit a state park, national park, national forest, or wildlife refuge in the last twelve months?*

- *On a scale of 1 to 5, 1 meaning not at all and 5 meaning very high, how would you rate your interest in the outdoors and the natural environment?*

- *On a scale of 1 to 5, 1 meaning not at all and 5 meaning very high, how would you rate your interest in the study of animals, plants, and nature?*

- *On a scale of 1 to 5, 1 meaning not at all and 5 meaning very high, how would you rate your interest in birds?*

- *Do you know anyone whom you consider to be a dedicated birdwatcher?*

- *If yes, how many dedicated birdwatchers do you know?*

African American Birder Research Form, Page 2

Interviewer: Determine if respondent identified in the Participation Module as someone who watches birds (Participant). If so, read the remaining questions in the left-hand column of the following table; otherwise, read the remaining questions in the right-hand column of the following table to every other non-participant.

You previously identified yourself as someone who watches birds. Do you use binoculars and a bird identification book to look at birds?

Here is a list of reasons why people might not go bird watching as often as they would like. Please indicate which of these apply to you by answering "Yes" or "No."

Not enough time.	*I am uncomfortable because sometimes I feel afraid in forest or other natural settings.*
1. Yes 8. Don't Know	
2. No 9. Refused	1. Yes 8. Don't Know
	2. No 9. Refused
Not enough money.	
1. Yes 8. Don't Know	*Are there other reasons why you might not go bird watching as often as you would like?*
2. No 9. Refused	
	1. Yes 8. Don't Know
No one to go bird watching with.	2. No 9. Refused
1. Yes 8. Don't Know	
2. No 9. Refused	*What are those reasons?* (Record up to two)
I feel unwelcome or uncomfortable at many outdoor recreation areas because of who I am.	_____
1. Yes 8. Don't Know	_____
2. No 9. Refused	

You previously identified yourself as someone who does not watch birds. Here is a list of reasons why people might not watch or study birds. Please indicate which of these apply to you by answering "Yes" or "No."

No interest in birds.

1. Yes   8. Don't Know
2. No   9. Refused

I don't understand why one would want to study birds.

1. Yes   8. Don't Know
2. No   9. Refused

Not enough time.

1. Yes   8. Don't Know
2. No   9. Refused

Not enough money.

1. Yes   8. Don't Know
2. No   9. Refused

No one to go bird watching with.

1. Yes   8. Don't Know
2. No   9. Refused

I feel unwelcome or uncomfortable at many outdoor recreation areas because of who I am.

1. Yes   8. Don't Know
2. No   9. Refused

I am uncomfortable because sometimes I feel afraid in forest or other natural settings.

1. Yes   8. Don't Know
2. No   9. Refused

Are there other reasons why you might not go bird watching?

1. Yes   8. Don't Know
2. No   9. Refused

What are those reasons? (Record up to two)

_____

_____

Appendix B

Birding Festivals

Teresa Benson

HUMANS HAVE CELEBRATED nature for a long time. The Native Americans celebrated the abundance of Mother Earth with dance and music. They celebrated the health and prosperity of the land and animals.

Recently, people have found the joy in organized events that celebrate birds. Across the country nature festivals have sprung up, bringing annual celebrations to the best nature showcases in America. Many of these started in the late 1990s, in tandem with the public's growing interest in nature tourism.

Birding festivals honor the birds that inhabit and migrate through particular geographic areas. There are over 100 birding festivals currently listed on the American Birding Association's Web site (*www.american birding.org*). Most bird festivals are scheduled to coordinate with peak migration or breeding time for certain species. They take place from Washington to Florida, and from Maine to California. There are festivals during every month of the year, ranging from one day to ten days, and providing opportunity for anyone to attend and learn about the excitement of birding.

Festivals are free of charge, with certain field trips costing a reasonable fee. Most are organized by volunteer groups interested in spreading their love for birds and also help local economies by attracting birders to the area to spend their vacation time and money. Some festivals are also cosponsored by local government agencies, businesses, and chamber of commerce groups in order to expand education opportunities, promote tourism, and increase local citizens' environmental knowledge of their communities. A common thread to birding festivals is the goal that participants come and enjoy the birds the area has to offer, and go away from the event with a greater appreciation and awareness.

Many festivals focus on a certain group of birds that either migrate through the area at a certain time or live in the area year-round. Hummingbirds, for example, are the popular subject of many festivals in Texas, Arizona, New Mexico, California, Louisiana, and Missouri. At a hummingbird festival, one can see hundreds of hummingbirds working to consume up to 500 ounces of sugar water (the equivalent of over forty cans of soda) each day at preset feeding stations. The Bald Eagle is the guest of honor at festivals in Alaska, Washington, Oregon, and Connecticut. Bald Eagle festivals are unforgettable events, with visitors seeing hundreds of eagles over a weekend; and it is not uncommon to see over two dozen eagles in a single tree. For over ten years, the Turkey Vulture Festival at Audubon's Kern River Preserve in Weldon, California, has provided entertainment every fall for tourists from all over the world. During this festival it is possible to see thousands of Turkey Vultures flying over this small mountain community. Over 30,000 Turkey Vultures are annually recorded migrating through this area.

Other bird festivals highlight the high diversity of birds in a certain locale, often during peak migration when birds are traveling south for the winter or north for the summer. Some festivals, such as the Kern Valley Bioregions Festival, also celebrate the diversity of wildlife habitats. The Kern River Valley is located in the southern end of the Sierra Nevada in California at the confluence of five major bioregions, or major vegetation zones. The Bioregions Festival in Kernville began in 1994 as a celebration of the high numbers of birds migrating through the area each spring. Many of the birds stay to nest and raise their young, while others continue north to find unoccupied breeding grounds elsewhere. Over 340 species of birds have been documented in the Kern Valley, with birders reveling in seeing over 200 different bird species in just one day of birding.

Although the primary attraction of the Bioregions Festival and many other bird festivals focus on viewing birds, they also offer many other opportunities and activities centered on enjoying the outdoors. Field trips are offered for wildflower and tree identification, geology, butterflies, Native American heritage, nature photography, reptiles, and traditional uses of plants. Many festivals have special seminars, workshops, and presentations to help participants learn more about their natural world. Often these events are designed for small groups to allow for hands-on learning about such things as binocular use, nature photography, feather identification, bird song identification, animal tracking, and much more. Many have opportunities for birders to purchase "birding gear," such as binoculars and field guides, and bird oriented jewelry and clothing. Educational exhibits are also popular, especially when live animals are in attendance. Raptor rehabilitation groups will often bring their "spokesbird" hawk or owl to increase awareness of the dangers that imperil birds. A face-to-face encounter with a hawk is not one easily forgotten by a youngster or adult. The promise of being close to a bird of prey has thrilled many a returning festival-goer.

The Bioregions Festival is more than birds. Over the years many musicians have performed in a small park in Kernville, including an all-female Celtic music group called "Mama's Midlife Crisis." Other music has included Andean folk, jazz, bluegrass, classical, and blues. The music is as lively and diverse as the birds and flowers being celebrated. Music draws people of different cultures and generations together in a common interest. At the 2005 Bioregions Festival, Nat Dove, an internationally recognized blues pianist performed as part of the Arts Ambassador program for the Arts Council of Kern County. In light of sharing his passion of music with others, Nat Dove stated, "I want people to listen, to get in touch with their own truths and stories."

The Art of Birding Festival in Carlisle, Indiana, encourages people to develop a passion for birds, and as a result, helps them "get in touch" with themselves. The participants learn to nurture with nature. Nature plays a major role in the balance between mind, body, and spirit. Connecting with the natural surroundings and the birds that live there can increase self-awareness and a new appreciation for the world. Nat

Dove's idea about people getting in touch with their passions is easy to apply to those who share with others their excitement for birding. They want to show how wonderful and enriching birding can be.

Bird festivals are an enjoyable way for the first time birder to be introduced to the sport of birding. Beginning birder workshops offered at festivals demonstrate practical tips and ideas to the novice, and give valuable insight on easy ways to remember a bird. First time birders like to hear what a bird says in human words. For example, the Mountain Chickadee sings for a "cheeseburger, cheeseburger," and the California Quail exclaims, "tequila, tequila!" The Barred Owl asks, "Who cooks for you? Who cooks for you all?" Relating a bird's song with our language makes birding fun and easy.

Some newcomers to birding have fallen into the sport by attending the all day birding extravaganza, often referred to as the "Big Day." These marathon events take place as part of the birding festival, and entail birding every nook and cranny of a predefined area from dawn to after dusk. The objective of the Big Day is to tally as many bird species as possible. From the first call of a predawn flycatcher to the evening hoot of a Spotted Owl, the Big Day has convinced many a novice bird student into becoming simply a "birder." It is not uncommon to tally over 200 birds in one day's time, especially during peak migration periods in the spring and fall. Experienced birders share their enthusiasm and knowledge as they lead Big Day events.

Bird festivals are for beginner and expert birders to meet and celebrate birding. What started as a backyard pastime can expand to a favorite hobby after attending a festival. With the festivals comes camaraderie and kinship to those sharing a similar interest. Bird festivals offer families the chance to enjoy the outdoors together while learning about the environment.

The diversity of our natural world is important, and so is the diversity of the people who come to learn and celebrate it. In a survey taken in 2001 of two different nature festivals in California, it was found the audiences were not culturally diverse. The Kern Valley Bioregions Festival was part of this survey and found to attract Caucasians at a rate of 90 percent. With a large Hispanic and other minority populations living nearby in the Central Valley, more outreach to minority populations must occur if diversity in festival participation is to be met. The survey also found that Caucasians comprised 85 percent of the participants at the American River Salmon Festival near Sacramento, California.

Recognition of the bird and animal species diversity highlighted at these festivals will only increase once we encourage a diversity of cultures and races to attend the events. The prime goal of most birding and nature festivals is to promote an appreciation and understanding of the natural world. Because of their charm and allure, birds are an effective introduction. It is amazing to see the delight of a first time birder holding a recently banded titmouse to be released. Feeling the heartbeat of a bird in your hand can capture your heart forever. Seeing a beginning birder watch a bright red Summer Tanager against a deep green cottonwood tree is a reminder of how birding can transform you in so many ways. Birds remind you of the good in our world.

The future of land conservation lies not with just a few, but all of the people in our country. Education is the key to appreciation. Without venues such as bird festivals and other outdoor nature activities, it is difficult to promote bird watching and educate about the value of birds. Festivals bring people from all cultures together to celebrate the natural world, each other, and the benefits a diverse world has for us all.

Bird festivals are for everyone. Witness the magnificence of a hawk in flight. View a "kettle" of Turkey Vultures boiling in the sky. Experience the delight of twenty hummingbirds buzzing just a few feet from you. Take a tour with a bird expert. Look into the eyes of an owl, and celebrate the wonderful world of birds.

For more information about a bird festival near you, be sure to visit the complete list of festivals at the American Birding Association's Web site, *www.americanbirding.org*.

Appendix C

Birding Tours
Bob Barnes

NATURE IS FLAT-OUT FUN to experience. The world is full of all kinds of life. Experiencing that life is a natural high available to everyone. Each year, more people view nature through birding tours. The following will help you evaluate and choose birding trips based on destination, length, style, and budget.

The most important part of an enjoyable and successful birding tour is the leader. No matter the size of the group, reputation of the company, cost of the trip, or destination, the leader makes the trip. A knowledgeable, enthusiastic, well-organized, and expert leader who matches your personality and / or values will make a trip memorable for you.

Be sure to find out as much about the trip's leader as you can. A pre-trip telephone interview with the leader or the company who employs the leader is well worth the cost. Many companies have photographs and full biographies of their leaders, but bios do not reveal personality. This is judgment in the most positive sense. Different leaders match well with different participants. It is essential to choose the leader best for you.

A good to great tour leader or company wants the customer to have a memorable experience and return again. They will work with you to arrange the tour that best fits your objectives, even if it means referring you to another leader within the company or tour with a different company altogether. Be clear with what you expect and want.

What Is a Birding and Nature Tour?

A birding and nature tour goes to a location or a series of locations to experience and enjoy the birds and other natural elements. Many tour destinations are to places known for diversity of life not found elsewhere. For example, Southeast Arizona has several species of birds, butterflies, mammals, and reptiles found nowhere else in the United States, and central Michigan is the destination for many in hopes of observing a single species, the Kirtland's Warbler. Antarctica is the destination for experiencing hundreds of thousands, even millions, of penguins of several species, and the indescribable beauty and variety of icebergs spawned by the South Pole's continent.

A tour may be conducted on your own, using a bird finding guide, with a volunteer, a small tour company, or a large tour company supported by a large staff and decades of experience.

Birding Tour on Your Own

Birding on your own has advantages when compared to formal birding tours. There is maximum flexibility with the length of the trip perfectly matched to your wishes including vacation days. The start and end of the day is entirely self-determined. The itinerary can change at will. You can linger at a spot to enjoy a wildlife sighting as long as you want. Mealtimes are conveniently moved up or delayed, and going to destinations not visited by tour companies is an option. Birding on your own is the most cost-effective as there are no professional services involved.

However, there are disadvantages. They are clearly shown by reading the advantages of using major tour companies later in this appendix.

Bird Finding Guides

For birding on your own, there are many bird finding guide books, especially for noteworthy birding areas in the United States. Securing a guide will help immensely with trip planning. The American Birding Association (ABA) has produced excellent guides to Alaska,

Southeastern Arizona, Arkansas, Southern California, Colorado, Florida, Michigan, North Dakota, Rio Grande Valley, Texas Coast, Virginia, Washington, Wyoming, the Bahamas, and metropolitan areas of North America. Falcon Press has also produced several bird finding guides.

Internationally there are guides to all or parts of Mexico, Central America, the Caribbean, South America, Europe, Africa, the Middle East, Asia, Australia, and Oceania.

Bird finding guides aim to provide information necessary for successfully enjoying your visit to the area. The most important part of every bird finding guide are the chapters on locations (for example, a National Wildlife Refuge) with specific sites to be visited in a logical order. These chapters include maps, detailed directions with mileage to the nearest tenth of a mile, sites described in detail, and the bird species and other wildlife to be expected. The nearest accommodations and eating establishments are often mentioned.

Many other items are also covered. The ABA's *Birder's Guide to Southern California* (see bibliography) covers geography, weather, when to come, what to wear, where to stay, suggestions for viewing wildlife, an annotated list of specialty birds of Southern California, lists of reptiles, mammals, and amphibians you may see, a checklist of birds with bar graphs showing abundance, habitats and months of the year to be found, and an index .

Magical moments can be had based on information provided by an accurate bird finding guide. Olin Sewell Pettingill, Jr. was one of the first to produce bird finding guides. I used his *Guide to Bird Finding: West of the Mississippi* published in 1953 (see bibliography), and followed the section on Wyoming's Yellowstone National Park to a campground on the Madison River to look for Harlequin Duck at the lower end of the island in the Le Hardy Cascades. There was a pair of Harlequin Ducks exactly where Pettingill recommended, magical enough, but the added magic was that my visit took place decades after the Pettingill guide was published. That specific experience of using Pettingill's book and finding site-faithful Harlequin Ducks still brings a smile to my face, adds joy to my life, and adds to the experiences I can share with others.

Hundreds of such experiences with nature have enriched my life and are there to be added to yours.

Birding with a Volunteer

The American Birding Association produces a directory with local contacts for members around the United States and elsewhere who will volunteer to take you birding in their local area. In addition to cost savings, these volunteers can take you to local birding hotspots not visited by the tour companies. They can take you out at any time of year, whenever you visit their particular area.

When I lived in Porterville, California, I was on the ABA volunteer list, and often contacted by ABA members who asked me to take them to look for California Condors and Black Swifts. These are two bird species coveted by birders. I took these birders to locations not on any tour company's itineraries, and likely never will be.

The advantages of this kind of tour are clear. You can take advantage of birding anywhere at anytime. If you plan a visit to a relative in, say, Little Rock, Arkansas, in mid-October, a pre-trip contact with an ABA member volunteer can result in fee-free birding with a person who knows the local area, often intimately.

Take full advantage of the services of local volunteer bird guides, especially during vacations, on short visits to relatives, during business trips, and while attending conferences. Combine local ABA volunteers with published bird finding guides, and a trip of any length, any time of year, to most any place, and the pursuit of birds and other experiences with nature are significantly enhanced.

Small Tour Companies

A small tour company has trips offered by individuals who operate on their own or with a small staff. Included are trips offered by local bird clubs or Audubon Societies.

Birding tours offered by small companies are usually more costly than self-guided tours, but they are almost always less costly than tours offered by major tour companies.

Most small tour companies know their local areas very well. After all, they live in and bird their local areas throughout the year. If the leader's personality matches with yours, a trip to their local area will likely be successful.

Trips offered to locations away from the leader's or small company's headquarters must be researched to see if they can deliver on expectations. The quality of small birding company tours varies from very poor to truly outstanding. Do your homework. See the guide advice at the beginning of this appendix. Here are some questions to ask:

- *What is your overall trip philosophy?*

- *How many trips have you taken to this destination?*

- *Will you be using local leaders?*

- *How many days will you be staying in each place?*

- *What is the quality of accommodations?*

- *What is the pace of your trips? When does the birding day begin and end?*

- *Can you supply a variety of references from past trips?*

- *How do you handle rest and meal breaks?*

- *What form of transportation is used?*

- *How do you insure that everyone has the best opportunity to see the wildlife encountered?*

- *When it is legal to do so, do you use tape playback to attract birds?*

- *Do you include all meals in your price?*

The above questions may be used with the major tour companies as well, even though their Web sites may answer them quite well.

To illustrate the above, I will use two recent trips I made to Costa Rica. The first was a disaster. The second was a trip I offered, so you will have to make your own judgment.

Example One: On a recent scouting trip to Costa Rica with one of my tour leaders and local tour operator / bus driver, I ran into a fund-raising birding tour to benefit a bird club in the United States. The trip was made up of ten members of the club. They were happy to be in Costa Rica, one of the great birding destinations and a perfect country to be introduced to tropical birding. Their leader was a friendly, kind, and enthusiastic staff member from the local organization. The trip cost was very reasonable and the itinerary of places to visit was outstanding.

The unraveling of the trip took place before me and my scouting companions. The leader did not know the birds, and they were wildly misidentified. Several days later, we ran into the group again on the other side of the island. The lack of expertise and accuracy had taken its toll. As participants had realized the lack of competence, they had turned on the leader. The list of birds seen was quite small, and the accuracy of the identifications was in question for numerous species. In order to save money, the leader had served as the driver and leader in a foreign country with narrow roads and not the most consistent signage, and a lack of birding experience and expertise. The result was a trip that produced long faces, unmet expectations, and a loss in confidence in a staff member who was clearly a good and well-intentioned person.

The options of going on one's own and hiring a local driver and guide or spending more money for a well-organized tour would have likely resulted in the trip of a lifetime these participants were seeking.

Example Two: Bob Barnes and Associates recently conducted two trips to Costa Rica, one in January and the other the following March. The January trip had participants who were generally interested in culture and nature. They did not consider themselves birders. The participants on the March trip were passionate birders.

Both trips covered fifteen days in Costa Rica with an optional extension to Tortuguerro National Park. Everyone was informed of the philosophy and style of the trip.

The trip was limited to twelve participants, an expert Costa Rican leader, an American co-leader, and a Costa Rican bus driver, Alberto Vargas, who operates his own multi-bus tour company, Vitratur, and is an excellent bird spotter and identifier. An air-conditioned, nineteen-passenger Toyota bus with a microphone and speaker system was used.

The cost of the tours was all-inclusive starting with pickup at the airport in San Jose, Costa Rica. All in-country leadership, transportation, meals, snacks, accommodations, entrance fees, and basic tips were covered. Purchase of personal items and souvenirs, optional tips for the Costa Rican leaders and extra services, as well as the $26 airport exit fee, were the responsibility of the participants. Three hundred dollars in spending money beyond the trip fee was recommended.

After twenty-plus years of organizing tours in Costa Rica and serving as a driver, Alberto knew Costa Rica from the inside out. Both Alberto and the Costa Rican leader spoke Spanish as their primary language and were also fluent in English.

Everyone was picked up by the trip's two leaders and Alberto at the single exit to the airport building and taken to their first night's lodgings. There was no need to wonder what to do next, and with the two Costa Ricans, there were no cultural and language barriers to overcome.

Some participants chose to come in a day early to acclimate or stay a day or two after the trip. Vitratur made hotel arrangements with the American leader, provided transportation from the airport to the hotel's front door, and made sure they got into their rooms.

In order to prevent unpacking and packing of luggage each day, the average length of stay at each accommodation was three to four days. Accommodations included air-conditioning, and swimming pools at most sites for afternoon and evening relaxation.

Meals were served on site, with freshly prepared foods served buffet style so participants could take what they wanted in whatever amounts and go back for more if desired. Participants said they couldn't imagine more excellent food over the course of two weeks on a comparable trip anywhere in the United States.

Since the January trip was made up of participants with general interests, Antonio Cedillos, a Costa Rican leader with expertise in several disciplines, was hired. Antonio had conducted monkey research for two years, and also worked on forestry research. He knew almost all of the birds of the country and had taken certification courses from

Costa Rica's tourism department. Participants raved about his expertise and outstanding personality. It no doubt helped that Antonio had ten years' experience as an official Costa Rican tour leader.

Due to the birding focus of the March trip, expert Costa Rican birder Gerardo Vega was hired as the primary guide. He had twenty-five years of experience in bird research and bird tour guiding, and was co-founder and president of the Costa Rican Naturalist Tour Guide Association. Gerardo was truly amazing at spotting birds, even through the thickest of jungle foliage. He knew most of the calls and songs of the birds, usually identifying them before we ever saw them so we had an idea of what to expect. A guide with a major American bird tour company stated, "Gerardo is one of the best birders in Costa Rica, and probably the best on the Caribbean side of the country. You are fortunate to have him as the primary leader of your trip."

The participants in the two tours said they had the trip of a lifetime. One person said he had been waiting to get to heaven, but he hadn't needed to wait. He found heaven in Costa Rica.

There are numerous individuals and small tour companies that conduct excellent trips. Always ask lots of questions and check several references before committing. If in doubt, go with one of the major tour companies discussed below. Bob Barnes and Associates recently received an inquiry about a July birding trip to Costa Rica. Having no such trip planned, an Internet search revealed that FIELD GUIDES, a major American bird tour company, was offering such a trip. Without hesitation, that company and trip were recommended. The only step remaining before committing was to check out the leader's personality and style with the company.

Major Tour Companies

Three companies based in the United States, Field Guides, Vent, and Wings, are included in the list of major tour companies. Each company offers over one hundred tours worldwide every year. Major tour companies offer several advantages when compared to other birding tour options.

All three companies have outstanding leaders, among the most famous in the world of birding. Think of the "all stars" for any sport. The major tour companies hire the birding world's all stars. These leaders are often the ones who wrote the books. They live and breathe birds and birding every day of the year, and communicate the latest advances in birding with each other. They often have a decade or more of birding at the destinations on the tour itinerary. Many companies offer their leaders for hire by individuals and private groups during non-tour days.

The tour leaders have extensive contacts to gather the latest local intelligence as to where to find a highly sought bird species during a particular time of year, season, or even time of day. For example, "Go down the trail to 100 yards past the large pond. If you are there between seven and eight in the morning, you will see Red-capped Manakins at their lek (mating display area). If you arrive after eight o'clock, they will be gone." The major tour companies usually see the greatest number of bird species on any trip.

Once you get to know the company and their leaders, you can plan for many rewarding trips. These companies offer over one hundred trips each year, and decades of experience in organizing and running tours to the world's major birding destinations. They are experts at handling the logistics. They know the best places. Either the leaders serve as the drivers, or have reliable drivers to take their groups around. They have refined their itineraries over the years and know the idiosyncrasies of each destination. Due to their large size and numerous customers, they continuously receive feedback from participants and act on it.

Major tour companies have professional catalogs that describe trips, leaders, and policies in detail. More than other tour groups, the major companies depend on providing an excellent product. Bird tours are their only business. They must meet expectations or they will not survive.

Field Guides was founded in 1985. They offer 100+ tours per year as well as customized trips for private groups of eight or more.

Victor Emanuel Nature Tours (Vent) was founded in 1976. They have 140+ tours per year, and are the largest company in the world specializing in birding tours.

WINGS was founded in 1973 for birding in Northeast United States, and expanded in 1980. They lead 100+ tours per year.

Every birder should take at least one tour with a major company. The experienced expert leaders, arrangements made for you, and visits to secret places make the experience among the best to be had. Tours with major birding tour companies do come at a price. They are usually priced higher than other tours of comparable length and destination. However, they are worth the extra cost. Personal budgets will likely determine the final selection.

Birding and Nature Tours for Beginners

A great leader is experienced and has good teaching skills, and loves to share their knowledge. The best leaders have excellent patience. Perhaps the favorite customer of a bird tour leader is a passionate beginner with a hunger for learning. Companies sometimes have trips designed especially for beginners. Ask tour company operators to recommend the most patient leaders and trips for beginners.

Beginners are the most prized customers because they are open to learning and much will be new to them. On my first trip to Southeast Arizona with the WINGS company, I saw seventy bird species I had never seen before. The customers after only a few species might not have had an equal trip to mine in terms of surprise, wonder, and excitement.

If you are a beginner, try a short, inexpensive trip first. Some tour companies offer field weekends where a particular group such as hummingbirds is studied. This is much less overwhelming than tackling all the world's birds at once. By participating in a focused workshop, you will become a relative expert on the topic presented in a brief time.

Birding and Nature Tours for Minorities

Although not proportional to the percentage of the overall population, there are birders from all walks of life, ethnicity, and religion. In urban areas, such as the San Francisco Bay region, minorities are more prevalent on birding trips and at nature festivals.

Minorities are encouraged to take up or expand birding and birding tour participation. The passion of birders and nature lovers for their avocation makes it an egalitarian enterprise. There is nothing like a shared passion to bring people together.

The passion for birds and wildlife is a great equalizer. It provides the focus for the group. Young or old, male or female, novice or expert, the passion serves to hold the group together.

In order to see the birds of the world, you must travel to all kinds of habitats. No other outdoor recreation draws its participants not only to high mountain and ocean vistas, but to swamps, grasslands, cliffs, meadows, ponds, lakes, deserts, salt evaporation ponds, and above offshore submarine canyons.

Birds are everywhere. Pursuing them will take you everywhere, great cultures encountered along the way, and a fine dining experience will await you at the end of the day. Music, language, laughter, museums, architecture, friendships, and many other life experiences are there to be enjoyed. There are even bird tours specifically designed to combine human culture and birding (see WINGS at *www.wingsbirds.com*).

If birds and nature stir you, participate in a birding or general nature tour. Your life will be enriched with memorable experiences.

Bibliography

Academy of Natural Sciences. *Birds of North America* series (Philadelphia, PA: Academy of Natural Sciences, 1992–2003).

American Ornithologists' Union. *American Ornithologists' Union Check-list of North American Birds,* 7th edition (McLean, VA: American Ornithologists' Union, 1998).

Barnes, Simon. *How to Be a Bad Birdwatcher* (NY: Pantheon Books, 2005).

Clements, James. *Birds of the World,* fifth edition (Temecula, CA: Ibis Publishing, 2000).

Cordell, H. Ken, Nancy G. Herbert, and Francis Pandolfi. "The Growing Popularity of Birding in the United States" (*Birding* 31(2):168–176).

Cordell, H. Ken, and Nancy G. Herbert. "The Popularity of Birding is Still Growing" (*Birding* 34(1):54–61).

Dunn, Jon and Kimball Garrett. *Peterson Field Guides, A Field Guide to Warblers of North America* (NY: Houghton Mifflin, 1997).

Ehrlich, Paul, David S. Dobkin, and Darryl Wheye. *The Birder's Handbook: A Field Guide to the Natural History of North American Birds* (NY: Simon and Schuster, 1988).

Farrand, John Jr. *The Audubon Society Master Guide to Birding,* three volumes. (NY: Alfred A. Knopf, 1983).

Kastner, Joseph. *A World of Watchers* (San Francisco: Sierra Club Books, 1988).

Kaufman, Kenn. *Birds of North America* (NY: Houghton Mifflin, 2001).

Kjelgaard, Jim. *Big Red* (NY: Holiday House, 1945).
Irish Red (NY: Holiday House, 1951).
Outlaw Red (NY: Holiday House, 1953).

Leahy, Christopher W. *The Birdwatcher's Companion to North American Birdlife* (NY: Princeton University Press, 2004)

London, Jack. *Call of the Wild* (NY: Macmillan, 1903).

White Fang (NY: Macmillan, 1906).

Louv, Richard. *Last Child in the Woods: Saving Children from Nature-Deficit Disorder* (Chapel Hill, NC: Algonquin Books, 2005).

National Geographic Society. *National Geographic Society Field Guide to the Birds of North America* (Washington, D.C.: National Geographic Society, 1987).

Peterson, Roger Tory. *A Field Guide to the Birds* (Boston: Houghton Mifflin, 1934).

Pettingill, Jr. Olin Sewell. *Guide to Bird Finding: West of the Mississippi* (NY: Oxford University Press, 1953).

Robbins, Chandler, Bertel Bruun, and Herbert Zim. *Birds of North America: A Guide to Field Identification* (NY: Golden Press, 1983).

Schram, Brad. *American Birding Association Birder's Guide to Southern California* (Colorado Springs, CO: American Birding Association, 1998).

Scott, Shirley L. *National Geographic Society Field Guide to the Birds of North America* (Washington, DC: National Geographic Society, 1987).

Sibley, David A. *The Sibley Guide to Birds* (NY: Alfred A. Knopf, 2000).

Stokes, Donald and Lillian. *Stokes Field Guide to Birds, Eastern Region* and *Stokes Field Guide to Birds, Western Region* by (NY: Little Brown, 1996).

Terres, John K. *Audubon Society Encyclopedia of North American Birds* (NY: Alfred A. Knopf, 1980).

Works used in chapter seven, "The Hard Facts"

Cordell H.K., G.T. Green, and C.J. Betz. "Recreation and the environment as cultural dimensions in contemporary American society," *Leisure Sciences* 24(1):13–41.

Floyd, M. "Race, ethnicity and use of the National Park system," *Social Science Research Review.* 1(2):1–24.

Gobster, P.H., and A. Delgado. 1992. "Ethnicity and recreation use in Chicago's Lincoln Park: in-park user survey findings," in Gobster, P.H. (editor), *Managing Urban and High-use Recreation Settings.* USDA Forest Service General Technical Report NC-163, Chicago, IL, pp. 75–81.

La Rouche, G.P. 2003. Birding in the United States: a demographic and economic analysis. Report 2001-1. Division of Federal Aid, US Fish and Wildlife Service, Washington, D.C.

National Survey on Recreation and the Environment (NSRE): 2000–2002. The Interagency National Survey Consortium, co-ordinated by the USDA Forest Service, Recreation, Wilderness, and Demographics Trends Research Group, Athens, GA and the Human Dimensions Research Laboratory, University of Tennessee, Knoxville, TN.

Robinson, J. C. "Relative prevalence of African Americans among birdwatchers," in Ralph, C. J. and T. D. Rich (editors), *Bird Conservation Implementation and Integration in the Americas: Proceedings of the Third International Partners in Flight Conference,* (Gen. Tech. Rep. PSW-GTR-191. Albany, CA; Pacific Southwwest Research Station, Forest Service, US Department of Agriculture, 2005), pp. 1286–1296.

Robinson, J.C., G. T. Green, and H. K. Cordell. "A comparative analysis of African-Americans' participation in bird watching," *Birding,* at press.

Washburne, R. F. "Black under-participation in wildland recreation: alternative explanations," *Leisure Sciences* 1:175–189.

Wauer, R. "Profile of an ABA Birder," *Birding* 23(3):146–154.

West, P. C. "The tyranny of metaphor: interracial relations, minority recreation, and the wildland-urban interface," in Ewert, A.W., D.J. Chavez, and A.W. Magill (editors), *Culture, Conflict, and Communication in the Wildland-Urban Interface* (Boulder, CO: Westview Press, 1993), pp. 109 – 115.

Index

About the Author

JOHN C. ROBINSON, renowned natural history tour guide and author of five books on birds, nature, and the environment, has been studying birds and birdwatchers since 1979. An African American ornithologist, John is an advocate for minorities in bird watching. For over twenty-five years, John worked as a wildlife biologist and professional ornithologist for the US Departments of Interior and Agriculture. He wrote all the species accounts and the computer code for his comprehensive multimedia program, the *North American Bird Reference Book* CD-ROM, which has received international recognition and has sold over 100,000 copies.

Information about the free trial of the *North American Bird Reference Book* CD-ROM that readers of *Birding for Everyone* are entitled to

PURCHASING THIS BOOK entitles you to a free trial of my *North American Bird Reference Book* bird-watching software, and to a substantially reduced price should you decide to keep it. The software is a full-featured, instructional multimedia CD-ROM that provides bird lovers everywhere with unlimited learning and entertainment opportunities. With 851 high-resolution photographs, natural history accounts for each of the 922 birds of North America, 415 bird songs, 627 range maps, quizzes, and an identification key, the software provides an array of instructional capabilities for the bird student who is interested in learning more about birds or improving his/her bird identification skills.

This product simplifies the process of learning about the wild birds around you and improves your ability to identify them, using customized quizzes that you yourself can easily create, and take over and over again. Imagine seeing a bird and then, just minutes later, reading all about its natural history and where it breeds, and seeing one or more pictures of the bird and possibly hearing its song!

The reference book has met with tremendous success since it was first released. Since 1999, nearly 100,000 copies have been sold worldwide. Teachers love it, and kids want it!

The *Reference Book* is the crowning achievement of my career as a professional ornithologist. It is produced for birders, by a birder. It is written in concise, easy-to-understand language. Since 1979, I have been helping others learn how to identify and appreciate birds. Now you, too, can benefit from my decades of experience in identifying and studying birds.

You can order your own free trial copy of the *Reference Book* using the order form on page 145. Although we ask for your credit card information, aside from a nominal shipping fee, your card won't be charged unless you decide to keep the software. Should you decide to keep it, your card will be charged the amount indicated on the form approximately 45 days after the product has been shipped to you. Otherwise, you can return the software within 30 days and owe nothing.

"Since our store opened we have had numerous requests for comprehensive birding software that not only includes bird songs [and] range maps, but at a price everyone could afford. Now we have it! LANIUS Software's North American Bird Reference Book... We have reordered several times in less than a month."

— Joanie Smith, East Bay Nature store, Walnut Creek, California

"My kids and nieces and nephews just love the North American Bird Reference Book by LANIUS Software on CD ROM. I wanted to have a computer game for my younger nieces and nephews to look at besides the complex and sometimes scary games my older teens play with. I bought the Bird CD and it turned out we all had fun with it! The younger ones love to look at the pictures and listen to the bird calls. The older kids love to go out on the hills in the back and look for birds, come back to the house and check out what they have found. They can do this for hours!...Thanks, LANIUS Software, for developing such a great nature and bird learning tool that I think kids all over would have a lot of fun with. Much better than some TV shows or other computer games!"

— Marilyn Chelini, Dublin, California

"Someone gave me the Bird Reference Book as a gift. My four-year old twins can sit for hours looking at the amazing quality of the bird pictures. The woodpecker is one of their favorites, since we have so many in our trees. Now when we go outside, they tell me all about birds. Why don't you sell this in schools?"

— Karen Robertson, mother of twins, Lafayette, California

"Once we discovered the fun bird photograph and song quizzes, we simply could not stop using the software; before we knew it, it was past 3:00 a.m. and we realized how easy it would have been to stay up all night playing with this wonderful software!"

— Larry Arbanas, California

Order Form
For free trial of Bird Watching Software

Please send me a trial copy of John C. Robinson's North American Bird Reference Book *multimedia CD-ROM. (Limit one trial copy per customer.) I understand that I may return the software within 30 days and owe nothing; otherwise, my credit card will be charged for the indicated amount approximately 45 days after On My Mountain, Inc. receives my order. The shipping fee is non-refundable.*
(If paying by check or money order, make check out to: On My Mountain, Inc.)

Product	Unit Price	Quantity	Total
North American Bird Reference Book CD-ROM	$19.99	1	$19.99

Please send more FREE information on:
❏ Other Books ❏ Speaking / Seminars
❏ Birding & Natural History Tours ❏ Consulting ❏ Mailing Lists

Name: _____

Address: _____

_____

City: _____ **State:** _____ **Zip:** _____

Telephone: _____

Email Address: _____

Credit Card Number: _____ **Expiration:** _____

Authorized signature: _____

Sales tax: 8.625% will be added for products shipped to California addresses.

Shipping by Priority Mail:

U.S.: $7.00 **International:** $10.00 (estimate)

Fax Orders: 707-402-6319. Send this form.

Telephone Orders: Call **707-688-2848**. Have your credit card ready.

Email Orders: info@onmymountain.com

Postal Orders: On My Mountain • 5055 Business Center Drive, Suite 108, PMB 110 • Fairfield CA 94534, USA. Send this form.

See the Quick Order Form on page 146 for ordering additional copies.

Quick Order Form

Other Books, Products, and Services by John C. Robinson

Fax Orders: 707-402-6319. Send this form.

Telephone Orders: Call 707-688-2848. Have your credit card ready.

Email Orders: info@onmymountain.com

Postal Orders: On My Mountain, Inc.
5055 Business Center Drive, Suite 108, PMB 110, Fairfield CA 94534.
Send this form.

Please send the following books, disks, or reports.
I understand that I may return any of them within 30 days for a full refund for any reason, no questions asked.

Product	Unit Price	Quantity	Extended Amount
Birding for Everyone – the book	$18.95		
North American Bird Reference Book CD-ROM	$64.95		
Secret of the Snow Leopard – science fiction novel	$16.95		
		Shipping	
		Sales Tax	
		Total	

Please send more FREE information on:

❏ Other Books ❏ Speaking / Seminars
❏ Birding & Natural History Tours

❏ Consulting ❏ Mailing Lists

Name: _____

Address: _____

_____

City: _____ **State:** ____ **Zip:** _____

Telephone: _____

Email Address: _____

Credit Card Number: _____ **Expiration:** _____

Authorized Signature: _____

Sales Tax: Please add 8.625% for products shipped to California addresses.

Shipping:

US: $7.00 for first book or disk; $2.00 for each additional product.
International: $11.00 for first book or disk; $5.00 for each additional product (estimate).